WALNUT STI

PAST, PRESENT AND FUTURE

An oral history of the Walnut Street area of Leicester

BY COLIN HYDE

CRASH ARTS LTD

Crash Arts Ltd has been working in Leicester since 1981. It was the first community arts project to be set up and has had a major impact on the arts in Leicester. The company offers a diverse range of skills to people who do not normally get access to arts activity. The idea for a documentary arts project came about through our local arts work. We have been undertaking a four year programme of work in the Walnut Street area, and were aware of the changes that had taken place in this community. Because of the close contact we have with local residents we know of the feelings that the City Challenge process is generating, and feel it is important to offer people a vehicle where their experiences and views can be heard. We hope that everyone involved in regenerating urban areas will find this book useful.

ACKNOWLEDGEMENTS

Crash Arts wishes to thank the following for their help in compiling this book:
All those who agreed to be interviewed; the staff of the Living History Unit who conducted many of the interviews concerning Bonners Lane; Leicester City Council who allowed access to plans and correspondence about the various stages of the slum clearances; Val Smalley.
We are also grateful to the following for permission to reproduce photographs: Leicester Mercury; Leicestershire Museums, Arts and Record Service; Mr Cook; Mr & Mrs Zientek; Mrs Howes; R. Hutchinson; C. Hyde. Particular thanks to Cynthia Brown for reading and commenting on the text.
We gratefully acknowledge the following for their financial assistance: East Midlands Arts; Leicester City Council; Leicester City Challenge Ltd.
Title page illustration by Roger Hutchinson.

FURTHER READING

This book forms part of a Documentary Arts project run by Crash Arts Ltd. As well as the tape recorded interviews (which now form part of the archive of the Living History Unit) Crash Arts has a large collection of photographs and documents relating to the Walnut Street area. These can be consulted by arrangement.
Additional information came from:
Nash D. & Reeder D. ed., *Leicester in the Twentieth Century* (1993); *Leicester Mercury*;
Frizelle E., *The Life and Times of the Royal Infirmary at Leicester* (1988); Badger B., *100 Years of Service, St Andrews 1862-1962*; *Leicester Chamber of Commerce, Year Book 1911*; Leicester City Council, *Development Plan* (1952); Kelly's and Wright's *Directories*; Read Jr R., *Modern Leicester* (1881); Old photos of the area around the Newarke can be found in Courtney P. & Y., *The Changing Face of Leicester* (1995).

ISBN 0 952 10908 5
© Crash Arts Ltd.
Designed by Creativity Works
Published by Leicester City Council
Living History Unit

CONTENTS

Introduction 5

What was the area like? 9

Houses... 15

A close-knit community... 23

Leisure 31

School days... 43

Walnut Street at work 49

Walnut Street at war 55

Shops 61

Demolition 69

The uncertainty of it all 79

Living in the area now 85

What do people want? 91

The junction of Walnut Street and Aylestone Road in 1964. This is now the Leicester Royal Infirmary car park. (Leicester Mercury)

INTRODUCTION

On the face of it the Walnut Street area of Leicester is a thriving, busy part of town. In one small area there is De Montfort University, the Leicester Royal Infirmary, Leicester City's football stadium, the Tiger's rugby ground, Granby Halls, Southfields College, and the canal. Nearby are the ancient Raw Dykes, the Gas Museum, Freemen's Common, Welford Road cemetery, the Jain Temple, and to the north, around the Magazine and the Newarke, part of what was Medieval Leicester.

Amongst all this the people who live in the area sometimes feel forgotten. With the huge amount of traffic passing through the area, students moving into many of the houses, and the St Andrew's estate being perceived as a magnet for trouble, residents often feel that they are a community under siege.

However, it wasn't always like this. Before the 1960s the Walnut Street area was a self-contained working class community. There were many factories and places of work as well as scores of small shops. The closeness of the small terraced houses gave people a feeling of security and made for a very strong sense of community.

The change came in the 1950s, when the older houses in the area were demolished as part of a slum clearance programme. It continued into the 1960s and 1970s as many streets were torn down to make way for the expansion of De Montfort University and the Infirmary, and the creation of the St Andrew's estate. In many ways the community never recovered from this upheaval.

In 1992 Leicester City Challenge was set up in an attempt to regenerate the area. However, local memories were still scarred with the trauma of the previous redevelopment and many people were very sceptical about what City Challenge were going to do. Now seemed a good time to review the history of the area and look at how it has changed.

This book is an oral history based on the memories of those who live, or have lived, in the area. It concentrates on what it was like to live in the community before the redevelopment of the 1960s, the effect the redevelopment had on people, and what it is like living in the aftermath of that development today. It also includes the opinions of people regarding the future of the area.

This book gives a fascinating and instructive insight into how redevelopment policies can change an area and the ways in which the people of the Walnut Street area have changed with it.

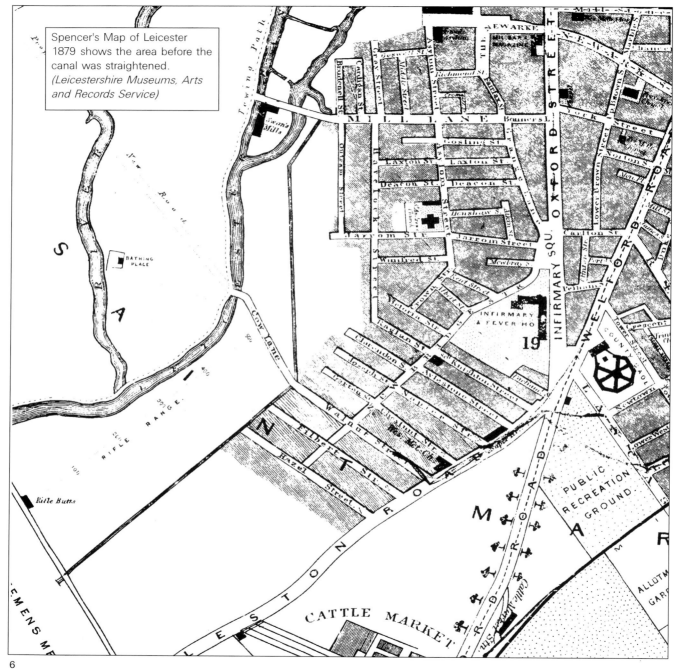

Spencer's Map of Leicester 1879 shows the area before the canal was straightened.
(Leicestershire Museums, Arts and Records Service)

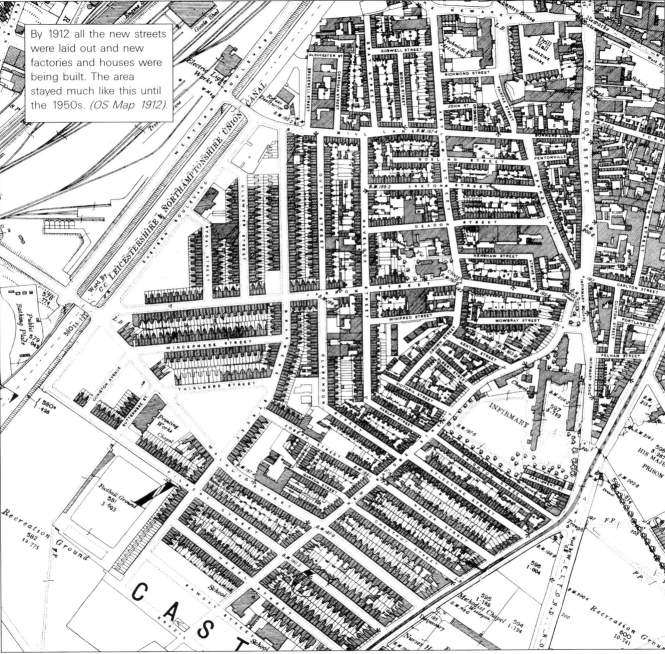

By 1912 all the new streets were laid out and new factories and houses were being built. The area stayed much like this until the 1950s. (OS Map 1912).

A Brief History

For the purposes of this book the 'Walnut Street area' is the area from the Newarke and the Magazine down to Brazil Street and the Raw Dykes, and from Aylestone Road and Oxford Street across to the canal. It is part of what was known as the South Fields area of Leicester. The oldest part of the area, north of Mill Lane, by the Magazine and the Newarke, was part of Medieval Leicester. Bonners Lane and Grange Lane (then Green Lane) also appear on early maps.

During the Civil War, in 1645, the King's men lined up along what is now Walnut Street and bombarded the city wall, which ran along Mill Lane, where De Montfort University and The Gateway School are now. Women and children helped to raise up defences using woolpacks. The women were also recorded as fighting – *'Their women, unmindful of the danger, continued to keep a steady fire from the upper windows of many a house. Others stood upon the rooftops and hurled slates at us below'.* The last part of this wall was demolished around 1914.

In the 18th century the Leicester Races were held nearby, the horses often having to *'cross turnpike roads belly-deep in mire'.* The races were moved to what is now Victoria Park when the South Fields were enclosed at the beginning of the 19th century. This enclosure meant that Leicester could expand to the south.

Although the Infirmary had been established in 1771 much of the building in the area happened after 1811. The prison was completed in 1828; Welford Road recreation ground was laid out in 1839; the first football match was played at Filbert Street in 1891; the Tigers leased the land for their ground in 1892; and the county cricket ground was on Aylestone Road from 1901 to 1946 when it moved to Grace Road.

Before the 1890s the canal had not been straightened, so there were few buildings to the west of where Havelock Street is now. Once the canal had been straightened there was room to build more streets. A member of the City Council describes what happened:

There was a big change in this area... the first public health act was in 1875 and that controlled the nature of buildings so all of these houses which were all built around the turn of the century, 1895 to sort of 1905 were of a much better standard than all of these... all the pre-1875 ones that were all knocked down in the slum clearance in the early sixties - that my department did.

This (Grasmere Street) was built as a result of the Grand Union Canal being constructed, because originally the river meandered across here and actually part of this land is made up of ground where the old river bed was, so pre-1900 some of that land didn't exist. The top end of Grasmere Street and the top end of Ulleswater Street was actually built on the old river bed.

WHAT WAS THE AREA LIKE?

Rough? – No!

The Walnut Street area was generally what might be called a 'respectable' working class community, although some parts were less respectable than others. There were gang fights in some of the pubs on Mill Lane in the 1920s and 30s. These gangs mainly came from outside the area, but a few streets around Mill Lane, including Pentonville and Gray Street, acquired a 'rough' reputation. The following memories reflect these different views of the area.

They were very poor those days. My grandparents they came from Stone in Staffordshire and when they were about to come... the pastor there said, 'You're going into a sink of iniquity,' and I think he was probably right as well, it was an awful area for drink and turmoil. There used to be a character known as Jenny Carter, she was like a man, she was very strong, take any man on.

It wasn't a rough area, no. The properties were rough but the people who lived in them weren't rough. My grandfather was a dyer, worked in the dye works. That area... was a big area for hosiery trade, you know, dye houses all that sort of thing.

I was born in Outram Street 1910. I remember Bonners Lane very well. It was quite narrow and my uncle had a corner shop at corner of Oxford Street and Bonners Lane, greengrocery, and then opposite was Rowsells the shoe factory. Many years before that my mother and father used to play on that area before Rowsells was built and they used to talk about playing in a tunnel which was blocked off. Whether it was a genuine tunnel or not I don't know but it has struck me recently that it could possibly have been part of a... 'Sally' point for soldiers emerging to go to the defences which were nearby.

And then along there towards my uncle's shop was a row of... very small dilapidated houses and I do remember a family living there who had rickets probably caused by malnutrition, most of the family were affected by it.

There was a fruiterers and grocery shop on the corner there called Harvey's, further down there was a

Harvey's shop on the corner of Bonners Lane and Oxford Street in the 1950s. *(Leicestershire Museums, Arts and Records Service)*

hairdresser, Ernest Blower. On the corner there was another grocers... there was a pawnbroker's shop corner of Grange Lane. The little shops, well I tell you this, the shops all round that area were over run with mice and rats. Everybody had a cat to catch them and traps and poison and everything.

Pentonville was just a cul-de-sac, no more than what, 40 - 50ft long and the houses on Oxford Street used to back onto the end of it. It was supposed to be a really rough area but it wasn't really, I never had any bother down there.

Small area known as Pentonville was at the back of Bonners Lane in Grange Lane. There was a public house at the corner known as The Alderman and between Grange Lane and Oxford Street was a back alley which... was twisted like a dog's hind leg... known as the Twizzle and Twine which is no longer there.

Then, further down the Lane were one or two old cottages and then of course there were Bishop Bonner's House which was at the corner of Fairfax Street. I remember it being a conglomeration of all medieval stone and patched up with bricks and it was used as an engineering works.

On the right was a street which is now gone called Fairfax Street, on that corner there was a tripe and trotters shop. Further down on the right was Smith's, they were hauliers and carriers. Further down Mill Lane there was shops, public houses... quite a number of little streets with one up one down houses you know, it was completely full of these tiny houses. It was quite a busy area in the '20s.

The houses around there - that was Fairfax Street that ran alongside it. Very mean little cottages I think you'd call them. Then you went round the corner into Richmond Street, just in Richmond Street was the school clinic. Most children, if they went to have their teeth done or had to use the school doctors, from all over the city, had to go to Richmond Street. There you joined up with Asylum Street, as it was - now Gateway Street - my grandad used to call it Loony Street. It was called Asylum Street because an asylum used to be there many years ago. Again they were all fairly mean houses - you understand what I mean by the term 'mean'? They were meaner than the ones in Clarendon Street, they were much narrower. All of the streets had factories within the streets. Nearly every street had a pub at the corner.

Bishop Bonner's House.
This was demolished in 1935.
(A. Herbert)

The destructor was at the very bottom of the canal. All the household rubbish was collected on very low vehicles and they went down there and emptied in the yard and the men were pulling all the rubbish down a fire... like a big manhole and they pulled all the rubbish down there. Tins put on one side, all metal, and outside next to the canal was a quay and there was a compression machine there that engulfed all the steel up and made it into big ingots... and barges used to come and load up with it.

Down Outram Street... about three quarters of the way down on the right you go down an entry there and there were some more cottages behind that, one up one down, and they were beautiful. About five of them - there might have been more I don't know - with that much garden in front of them and flowers. It's unbelievable to have a street like Outram Street with these little places at the back with these little flowers in.

That was a very narrow street Outram Street, very overhanging and they were these tiny little houses built, you know, pre-1875. They were very much smaller, they didn't have passages between the bedrooms so you had to go through one bedroom to get to the other bedroom. Outram Street seemed to be much poorer.

It was a poor area, yes, the community spirit was good all around there. Where I lived (Outram Street) it was particularly strong really, any event of national importance or whatever they were always ready to celebrate, even dragging a piano into the street and dressing up... and singing.

In those areas, very close indeed, you could sense it. Everyone was willing to help out in some way shape or form, if anything unfortunate happened to anyone in their particular radius they were all there... they couldn't be more generous. Wonderful spirit in those days and that's what's been lost in this post war development you see, they've moved people out, they've broken up communities.

> ### Asylum Street
> (now Gateway Street)
>
> *Asylum Street where there used to be the asylum on the corner. It wasn't in my day but one always used to walk past it a bit warily, you know, the old tales of, like, ghosts used to be in, things like that. They were much older properties.*

Everything were clean and polished

Status was not just a matter of where you lived, but how you behaved.

Everywhere were clean and polished. It always struck me that all the steps were clean... well you did, automatic, you just did it. Everybody did. You seen them, all the old ladies kneeling on the mats cleaning everywhere outside, 'cos as I say it were very dusty, the door knockers shone. There was a smell wasn't there, a smell of cleanliness, you know, like soap if you like.

If you came into Clarendon Street all the front steps were scrubbed and the window sills. And you swept your front and when it snowed all the fronts were cleared. In fact, as kids we went round when it snowed and did snow sweeping for people - not free, I mean we never did anything for free. We always got paid for it, we were enterprising. Nobody left their front unclean. It was considered it was your obligation, I'm sure that's all it was - same as it was in the town - shopkeepers always cleaned their fronts. I think people had a sense of civic responsibility no matter what social status they were in.

There was definitely a hierarchy in the area, as I saw it as a kid... If you lived in new Clarendon Street you were a bit better than the old Clarendon Street, if you went over to Havelock Street you were going down the scale, and Raglan Street you were going down the scale. Getting further up toward the hospital, you were definitely going down the scale at the top of Crown Street. Come the other side of Clarendon Street moving over to Grasmere Street, Windermere Street and all those other streets you were going up in the scale - in the working class scale that was. So you talk about class structure, there was a very big class structure within the ordinary working people.

It wasn't an overt thing, it wasn't a thing that people said, 'I live in a better street than you', it was just accepted that if somebody wanted to move on and they wanted to better themselves, if they moved into Windermere Street they were bettering themselves. Gray Street and all of those streets were almost Wharf Street class - as I recall. Wouldn't go up there, no.

Grasmere Street was a relatively wealthy street I think. There's a chap that still works for me now who lived in Ullswater Street and he still refers to Grasmere Street as being the big houses, you know, and they were tiny little houses weren't they? We didn't have bathrooms originally... we had a back bathroom extension built in about '62 even, maybe as late as that. So I suppose we were poor but frankly we never noticed it.

It was quite a nice area to live I think. My sort of first memories really were of the changes probably, or the demolition, because the street at the back of us was demolished and the Poly sort of expanding rapidly. The little corner shop... that used to be one of my favourites, Bowles' shop on the corner disappearing. That was a general store, haberdashery sort of, hardware, everything from a mousetrap upwards he used to sell. It was a lovely little shop that was.

Certainly Grasmere Street was a great community. But we were probably a bit self-contained I think really... within the stretch from Mill Lane to Jarrom Street, that was our community and it wasn't outside of that. We knew everybody there intimately within that, literally everybody. All ages... very mixed bag. Very static community, been there a long while, still is to a great degree to be perfectly honest. There's probably 25% of that stretch there now occupied as student houses but the other 75% I bet were there when I was born. Progressively it became a less nice place to live, to be perfectly honest.

I remember the Fox's Glacier Mints factory quite well because we used to walk down York Road and there was this overpowering smell of Fox's Glacier Mints almost the whole area.

The Magazine

Where the underpass is now used to be an army barracks, did you know that?

In the Magazine there was a territorial army drill hall, a big square there where they used to have parading. There was a bus station there as well... Midland Red to Wigston there, on the Newarkes.

The Dewdrop Inn,
Laxton Street.
(M & J Zientek)

The Newarke Tavern,
Mill Lane.
(M & J Zientek)

HOUSES

Killing the bugs

The quality of the housing in the area varied greatly. Some houses around Bonners Lane had been built in the late 18th century, while others around Brazil Street were built in the 1930s. Even in one street there could be several different types of house. This man was a rent collector in the mid-1930s. He describes conditions in some of the poorer parts of the area:

Pentonville - one went down Bonners Lane and turned left into Grange Lane and the first entrance on the left was Pentonville. Now you went in through an open gateway and what fronted you were about four or five houses on the left and about four facing you and down the other side I have an idea there was a toilet block of either four or six closets. Now in the middle of this open space there was a common water tap and this open space was cobbled so in the winter it must have been desperate. The whole aspect was dull, grey and mucky. Overall the rents for these properties were round about two and nine a week which was less than 15p these days. I think they had two bedrooms - I only went upstairs once. There was a women there who had two kids. Generally this woman was in, you opened the back door - you just gave a cursory knock and in you went you see. Now inside it was all grey, brownish, and light coming through a very mucky window, underneath the window was the sink.

I went in there one morning in the late winter and she said, 'My roof's leaking.' She opened the front bedroom door... and again it was grey... it was a double bed and that was sort of... again I'll use the word grey because that's the only way you could see it really, it was all grey-white. I don't think the sheets had ever been boiled or anything like that. It'd got blankets on plus a couple of coats - there was no heating in the bedrooms. It'd got electric light downstairs but I have a feeling that the kids had to take candles to bed. I reckon they were built very late 18th or very early 19th century - rising damp and all the rest of it. She walked over to the far corner of the room and said, 'There it is... you can see it's very wet indeed.' As I turned to go out I looked round the walls and there were long red streaks coming all down the walls you see so I said, 'Have the kids been trying to do some decoration?' She said, 'What do you mean?' I said, 'All the streaks down the wall.' 'Oh,' she said, 'the kids have to kill the bugs every night before they get into bed.'

If you did come across a child in that circle where the properties were very old, full of bugs... he or she would either have bug marks on their hands or on their face even.

But again, you'd move into a house two doors away, it'd be as spick and span and you could eat off the kitchen floor, and that was the difference. Whether the difference was because the spick and span people were in work and the others weren't... you do think so but it doesn't always follow.

Now moving out of Bonners Lane and Pentonville down to the houses in Middle Street, Deacon Street, Laxton Street, Clarendon Street, their rents were higher, they

Pentonville was one of the oldest and most run down parts of the area. *(Leicester Mercury)*

It must have been hell

There used to be some houses round there, well when they demolished them I couldn't believe - they'd got 24 houses on that plot. Called Pentonville. You wouldn't believe. It must have been hell living in a place like that.

were round about... they varied from five shillings (25p) a week up to seven shillings (35p) a week. The bulk of tenants generally looked after the inside of the properties and anything wrong with the exterior fabric was done by the landlord. I didn't know the landlords because I was working for the estate agency but if work wanted doing then generally the landlords authorised it, because it was in their interest to keep the property in good condition, apart from this very old stuff which was fronted by Pentonville and Bonners Lane because that really was pretty grim. I think in Pentonville there must have been eight or ten cottages or houses and I reckon there were only six lavatories - they were outside. Bonners Lane and Pentonville were grim, very grim indeed, even in those days they were grim, they really were. How on earth people lived in them, looking back, I really don't know. They were living in a sort of time warp because they knew that nothing would ever improve - not so far as they were concerned... and yet underneath all that there was the fact that if any neighbour was in difficulty, sickness, anything like that at all, they'd be the first to help - and that to my mind is human nature at its best.

When you talk about the property on Bonners Lane, the coal house in the living room - you know that do you? There was no cellar. You went in off the street into the living room - there was only the one room - and the coal house was under the stairs, then there was a pokey kitchen, then

 you went out of the kitchen into the yard and the tap was also across the yard, the communal tap that everybody used. It was three storeys and when you went up into the one bedroom you had to go through that bedroom to get into the next one. My aunt lived there until they were pulled down... they moved them up to New Parks into pre-fabs, that sort of thing.

Housing on the corner of Grange Lane and Bonners Lane just before demolition in 1955. (*Leicester Mercury*)

I was born at 69 Asylum Street which was the corner of Asylum Street and Laxton Street... in a fish and chip shop. Next door was a grocery shop, Smith's, next door to that was a sweet shop and next door to that was a drapery.

It was a big house, yes, we'd got four bedrooms and we'd got a cellar. Down the cellar, you could go down steps from the pantry which was where the dining room was... you could go down the steps just as you come in the back gate, because we had a kitchen that led right away but it was under a glass roof, like a conservatory. There was nowhere round there that's got one. My brothers... used to do lantern slides down the cellar.

The shop front was quite big. You'd come in from the dining room into the shop at the back you see.

My elder brothers, they did a round, they'd got two horses and a big dray sort of thing and they used to move stuff for people that wanted it moving and they also had... two horses and people sat up on... used to take people to Bradgate Park and on outings. They used to come in the big gates that were in Laxton Street, cross the yard into the stables and then, above the stables, there was a hayloft. Facing, in the yard, was the forge where my father, he let that, they used to do candle sticks and all sorts of things. And above he used to let - boys, my brothers' friends and that, he bought them a snooker board - and he used to let them come and play up there.

Sweeping out the Cockroaches

These two ladies lived in different houses on Victoria Street, which was where the Infirmary's chimney is now.

I was born in number ten Victoria Street. Two up two down and then a huge community yard with one tap. I always remember the one tap because we had the floods once and we all stood watching the tap disappear. I think there was about six houses in ours. There was about four toilets - a block of toilets at the top of the yard and the wash houses up there where you used to have to take your washing. We used to have to sit and watch if you wanted to go to see if anybody was already in there and wait for them to come out before you could go in. Wasn't very nice believe me.

The thing I remember... it used to be overrun with cockroaches... it was a horrible place! But it was home, we didn't know any different. Dad and I used to have to go in and sweep the cockroaches out before my mum and Irene would go in in the evenings. And then when we moved to Aylestone Street with three bedrooms, well, we were living in luxury then weren't we. Still never had an indoor bathroom nor hot water.

Thunder Boxes

I'd got an aunt that lived in Gosling Street actually and that was just a basic two up two down, they hadn't got a cellar. The outside loos, there was two between the six houses and they used to fascinate me because they weren't... they were the old box type, I think they used to call them Thunder Boxes - a huge, like, box with a hole in. The sanitation was really rough... quite ancient loos. The houses were in a pretty rough state down there.

I was born in Victoria Street. 1921. It were quite a nice house really. Two bedrooms, two downstairs, and the kitchen was, you went across a little yard into the kitchen... the kitchen was separate from the house. You'd go out the back door and you'd go into the kitchen over there... and then you went down the side for the garden. Then there were six houses in the yard and there was two houses to each toilet with three toilets.

Being an end house my dad put a gate up. You went out that gate, you went past another two houses where you come to the entry, and that way you go to the toilets. You had to go down this yard, right down that yard, round again and round into the toilet. There would be many a night I took a candle holding my hand round it, stop it going out 'cos it were so dark... there were no lights there or nothing. I mean, nowadays you wouldn't live like it but them days they'd got no choice, me duck. The two neighbours are supposed to take it in turns but my mother used to do it most of the time. She used to scrub that seat, it were one of them wooden seats you know.

You hadn't got any heat, me duck, only in the living room. In the bedroom she'd got a grate but the only time the fire was lit in there, when my mother went in there when she was ill, then they had a fire in the bedroom but that was the only time. But there was no heat or anything in the backroom. My mother had got a gas mantle in the front bedroom but there was none in the back bedroom, you'd got no light at all, there were no light on the stairs.

They were happy days, me duck, I mean, you just can't believe now that your mothers and fathers managed the way they did, in the houses that there were. When the houses were in Victoria Street... the houses in Raglan Street, they backed up to you and when they were in their bedroom or even standing on anything in the living room they could see into your house. See there were no real privacy.

Not mice as such, I mean I sat with my mum one night and I looked down and there were a white mouse sat there. It were sitting at the side of the fireplace having a warm. But you used to get cockroaches, oh you used to get cockroaches, they were terrible. Where they used to come from God in heaven knows. In the cupboard, in the living room, you'd open that and yuck! I can't stand them.

Nice for starters

The area had several houses with just one room upstairs and one room downstairs. Often tucked away behind other houses in courtyards these were the smallest, cheapest houses in the area.

You know these little cottages near my mum, they were only one up and one down. That were at the bottom of Victoria Street. Ever so small they were, you couldn't swing a cat round in them. The one that my sister had when she was married... you used to say it was nice for starters in them days, 'cos you were lucky to get a house, me duck. I mean, when we was married, me and my husband, you couldn't get houses, I couldn't even get a photographer... wartime you see.

Some of the worst houses were one up and do you know I went in some of them? Do you know, it was fascinating. When you got a little passageway with a gas lamp behind ours and it was called Garton Terrace and they were one up one down. I'd never seen anything like that in my life, and yet they were spotlessly clean. You couldn't call it a kitchen. The tap was outside in the yard for all of them, about six of them, whatever. Where I went in them there were families of only twos or threes. I was shocked... that a woman could manage to go to work as well as manage to wash and keep children clean and cook. They all had gas stoves by the way. I never found any slums, let's put it that way. On the odd occasion you did have er... particularly the females - the men were quite happy whatever job they were doing to come home at night to a meal and things and didn't seem to worry about it so much - but the women would say, 'I think I'll be glad when we can go into a nice house where there's a bathroom and everything.'

I didn't come into this area until I was 16 when I got married, 1955. My husband came from this area, Outram Street. I think I preferred it then than I do now. You'd got all the community spirit, people were very friendly... the shops, you didn't have to go out of the area, you'd got everything you could possibly want.

The one I moved into, it was in a courtyard in between Outram Street and Havelock Street. It's at the back of a pickle factory, Drivers, and it was just a one up one down with a little kitchen thing. You'd got your cooker on one side and your sink the other and your coal house was underneath the sink... really good, really nice little places, it's just the way things were then. My mother-in-law lived just up the street, she'd got a three bedroomed terraced.

No bathrooms, still had the old tin baths. At that time, being 16 and married, I thought it was just my own little home and just made it as nice as we possibly could. It did seem a bit strange not having, you know, the extra space. But at the same time you didn't feel left out of anywhere or isolated like you do now, everybody rallied round, you know.

You didn't need to move very far in your kitchen, you hadn't got counters or anything, your draining board was at the back of the sink... and underneath the sink you'd got a couple of doors there where the coalman delivered his coal. The other side, you turn round you'd got your cooker so it was only like a small square. Surprisingly enough they were quite light, yeah. They were very warm, simple reason you'd only got the one room to heat downstairs. With the chimney stack being there you kept your bedroom warm as well. The only thing was coming down in the mornings to make the fire.

The only difficulty I had with the one up one down was the pram. 'Cos they weren't the small push chairs like you've got now, they were big coach built prams and... where to put that? You had to keep it in the living room. 'Cos there were no outsheds or whatever where you could put anything. The living room was big enough to have a couple of armchairs, we'd got the table... the sideboard - the usual dining suite. That's all we needed really. Full bedroom suite. When I look back they were quite roomy really... I don't think you'd be able to get a three piece suite in there as such. Your stairs came off your living room so you'd got one, two, three doors into one room. Your front door, the door to your kitchen - you know, the little bit of kitchen you'd got - then your stair door. But the majority of people blocked off the front door.

Well there was some damp, yes, I will admit there was some damp because you'd got the condensation. With it being so closed in you'd got your kitchen right next door to your living room and your backdoor and in the winter you'd got to have it closed obviously and of course the steam coming from there when you were doing any washing or you'd got anything cooking, you'd get the condensation and it did cause a lot of damp. Mainly on the inside wall where the little bit of kitchen was. Actually the sink came underneath the stairs, it sort of fitted under the stairs.

I had a... large big round tub thing with a lid on to boil nappies up and things like that. Always once a week you gave your whites a good boil and that caused a lot of condensation, sometimes you had to have the kitchen door open even if it was winter, otherwise you'd have been clouded out with steam. At the time... it (the rent) was twelve and three (61p) a week. It doesn't sound a lot now but then it did seem quite expensive.

The 'Nuts'

Knighton Street, Aylestone Street, Napier Street, and Chestnut Street were where the Infirmary car park is now. Half of Filbert Street and Hazel Street were demolished in the 1970s to make way for the nurses' flats. These people describe some of the houses in that area.

Aylestone Street was, it was a little bit posher than most 'cos we'd got three bedrooms and the smaller back room actually went over the old entry. So we got the front room which was always the posh room, then you got the living room and the kitchen. The kitchen had got running water but no hot water facilities and for some unknown reason, right up I think to the '50s, we'd got a gas light would you believe in the kitchen - the whole house had got electricity but the kitchen was gas lighting. We were quite lucky actually, we only had to share our loo with the people next door, which was an outside one and it wasn't one right at the bottom of the garden. That presented its problems obviously in the winter... the darn thing always used to freeze up.

I can vaguely remember there being like shutter things at the windows which my father used to religiously put up and it goes back to the war time and the days of the blackout, and I believe a lot of people in the area used to do the same right up to late '50s early '60s. Basically what it used to be was a frame that they used to put up at the old sash type windows and they just used to put a couple of catches on so no one could see from the outside.

The house as well had got a cellar which was divided into two parts - one where the coal used to come down... and the other half used to house the gas and electricity meters. And there was a hole in the wall which led through to the cellar of the house next door because I believe during the war they had a shared air-raid shelter which in actual fact was on the front... it was basically a brick thing with like a huge concrete slab on the front. On the front of the house itself - it was in the street, yeah.

We hadn't got any bathroom facilities or anything like that. The house I suppose was a reasonably dry house - there were lots of damp houses and things. The property belonged to the Royal Infirmary who were not particularly good landlords, they owned the lot. Some were quite different. The house next door must have been a workshop in its day, it had got like a... garage opening I suppose and two large double gates. A little further up the street there was six houses with an entry in the middle and they were not so well off as us, they had only two toilets between six and two taps which were out in the yard. The houses did vary and if I remember rightly the further up the street you got towards Granby Halls the posher they were, in fact I think there was a couple with bathrooms.

There were two standards of houses in Filbert Street. There was the top end which is still there now, they were quite nice houses, then it came onto the... in between New Bridge Street and what we knew as Grasmere Street (now Burnmoor Street). They were pretty well four houses to the entry... two either side. One toilet at the bottom for two houses. Smaller, yes, slightly, and they also didn't have running water. There was a pump at the bottom of the entry. In fact I can just remember we had a pump in our kitchen, that was the means of getting water, not tap water but a pump. It's unbelievable isn't it - what would that be? - 77 years ago. Front room, living room, kitchen, and three bedrooms. It was cold in the winter... I've been to bed many a time with a brick taken out of the oven wrapped in a towel instead of having a hot water bottle.

The Infirmary and the 'Nuts' in 1968. Going up the page, Aylestone, Napier, Chestnut, Walnut, Filbert, Hazel, and Sawday Streets. (Leicester Mercury)

We went down one day and just bought it (a house in Walnut Street in 1960). Went into Anleys, they were the people... I'd got £80 in my pocket, I thought we won't get a house for that and the lady said you've got plenty of money. That's how much we put down on a house in them days. It were massive really, it'd got a front room and a backroom and a scullery and then something else after that, a wash house... and the toilets were outside. It were like a dream to us. At the time we had to put in a pantry because all the people in them houses put all the foodstuffs on the top of the cellar steps... course when the coalman came they had to take everything out... because of the dust. I think it was £6 a month, the mortgage, and that was a lot of money then. It was our price bracket, that's why we bought the house, it was a start for us.

On the way to church. Jarrom Street and St Andrew's church in 1958.
(Leicester Mercury)

A CLOSE KNIT COMMUNITY

Getting on

Most people remember the area as being very pleasant and welcoming, and most will tell you they could leave their doors open without any fear of crime. However, as some of these quotes show, this was not true for everyone.

We didn't live in each other's pockets but as you can well understand they were house to house to house to house - you either got on or, well, as far as I know we got on.

There was usual doorstep gossip. In the summer you'd sit on the doorstep gossiping, summer nights, it was a common thing. If anyone was ill... there was always someone to help.

You talk about a close knit community, it had got its good side but it had also got some bad sides... because everybody knew what your business was before you did yourself. But they were always helpful.

It's quite funny actually because, the whole area (Aylestone Street), I think I'd say that everybody more or less knew everybody, if not by name by sight. In those days it was a much closer knit community and it covered quite a big area. I suppose actually the whole area from Jarrom Street right down to Hazel Street including perhaps Grasmere Street and all round there - it's quite a big area. There were a number of streets such as Gosling Street... and Laxton Street which all came into the area really, I think the reason being was that most of the kids went to Hazel Street school.

It was a community in which you lived, you worked and you played, and you shopped, it was all there, that's really what it was all about. I didn't realise, I honestly didn't realise I don't think until I was in my teens that there was anything but terraced houses. I wouldn't have known what a semi-detached house was anyway.

> ### Large Families, Small Houses
>
> *Two families at one house, 'cos there was no council houses. Being with my brother on the bread van he'd do the back, I'd do the front, that's how I know a lot of people lived two families to the one house... the 1920s. I knew families, one used to live next door, an old school pal of mine... I think his mother had twelve. They lived in a two up two down in Crown Street. If you'd seen one you'd seen the lot, all got a laugh on their faces.*

I think it was better than these estates - because everybody knew everybody, you could leave all your doors open, you needn't lock them. My mother had a back door key... you didn't need to. We didn't have anything to take, perhaps that's why, we'd no videos, things like that.

We never considered ourselves poor - you didn't think about it. Okay, you'd see kids with their backsides out of their trousers and the shoes with holes in, but you didn't think about it.

There was such a comradeship... You see, you kind of shared everything. When I had my children after I were 21, there were quite a lot of people having them at that age but they were fortunate, they'd got parents that would look after their children, and they'd got used to going to work during the war and they didn't want to give up so there were the two of them working, they used to often pass clothes onto people that hadn't... or they used to say I've got three or four frocks... or skirts, I'll let you have them for ten bob (50p). Well, you were grateful. It was neighbourly, people were very friendly then, they weren't trying to keep up with the Jones sort of thing or be one better than anybody else. Everybody was in the same boat and that was it. Then again if you did have a row with anybody during the day you could bet... that by the evening you'd be talking again.

In them days they all used to help one another, there was no back-biting or anything, only the one next door to my mum's, she were terrible, oh she were nasty. One woman set about her and had a fight once 'cos she were so nasty. She always used to go out and get canned to the wine, absolutely pickled like walnuts. They... brought her home on a barrow one night 'cos she couldn't find her way home. She walked in my mother's front door one night 'cos she'd lost her way - 'cos in them days you never locked your doors, you used to leave all your doors open and everything. She said, 'Oh I'm in the wrong house.' People used to have a drink and that but they never used to get like that.

It was a different age and people had different attitudes you know - you were all the same - I mean no one would think of locking doors or anything like that. When the milkman came round they'd probably leave the money on the table and the milkman would help himself.

We all talked to our neighbours. There wasn't this hopping in and out of doors that, you know, you hear about in probably further up north, you didn't leave your door open, you did lock your door because we did have robberies. I can remember us having a burglary, this was during the war. It was half term... the house had been broke into... twenty two shillings (£1.10) was taken out of the meter. The kids were caught - they lived in old Clarendon Street. A year later almost exactly the same thing happened but that time the kids got in and they absolutely ransacked the house, they found food and threw it all round the house, eggs and tins of tomatoes and things were thrown all over, and they took thirty seven and six (£1.88) out of the meter. Just the money and wanton damage. You hear about things going on today and people saying things aren't the same - it happened, it happened.

I do remember when we went on holiday my father going round the windows with a screwdriver and screws to fasten the windows down so no one could sort of get in.

There used to be one of the old blue police boxes which was opposite the Granby Halls. The police box, the public loos, and in between the public loos was the park keeper's - it was quite posh actually - it wasn't a hut it was part of the building. There was - I can only describe it as a huge great big shed on the other part of the park where the courting couples used to go... there was usually a policeman hanging round this police box if you needed one.

Home life

In the 1930s many front rooms, only used on high days and holidays, had an aspidistra in the window, and there were certain routines, such as doing the washing on Monday and having a bath on Friday, that were common to almost everyone.

Kitchen had a copper, which I can remember my mother used to do the washing on a Monday. We used to light a fire in this copper and it used to fascinate me when it had all gone cold because the copper would be full of like this horrible jelly substance which all had to be emptied by hand and taken outside.

A copper in the kitchen that you had to light a fire under to get it going. Washday was a full day. You had to punch them in the tub, boil them in the copper, blue them, starch them. My mother used to be at it when I went out of here to school, half past eight, and she was still at it when I came home half past four. I don't know as I'd like to go back to them. It was hard going, I mean, everything is so easy for them now.

On a Friday night the copper was put on, the water was filled into the copper and the fire was lit, and the tin bath came in from outside into the kitchen and we filled the bath and we all had a bath, you know. I always sat there with a flannel over my willy in case my sisters came in. We all used the same water, oh yes.

Friday night were bath night, the old zinc bath in the kitchen. We kept it in the shed, brought it in here, walls streaming and all wet and damp. I were the last one so I had all the clearing up to do. By the time I were that sweaty I wanted another bath.

The old range in here where... you had the fire in the middle, a tank at the side that held water for you to boil... for your hot water, and this side, two ovens. It was black and you had to black lead it every Friday. But, ooh, the stews you used to have in here. You used to put them in them earthenware pots and have them in there all morning. They were beautiful, your rabbit stews.
Every Friday night before we had baths you had to clean all your knives, 'cos your knives and forks weren't like they are today, they had to be cleaned. And we all sat round, one putting the stuff on and the other rubbing it off. Then at the side you had your coal bucket with your coal in and your tongs and your big poker. They were brass, they had to be cleaned... with Zebo it was called, quite a strong smelling stuff really, liquid... virtually like cleaning your shoes. You put it on with one brush you rubbed it off with another.

At the corner of Aylestone Street and New Bridge Street was a coal yard where we used to fetch the coal. The chap would put a hundred weight of coal in a timber trolley, it was a high side... with big wooden wheels and an iron bar... and we had to trundle this up and then manoeuvre it down the entry and into the backyard and then off load it and take the trolley back. That's how we used to get our coal.

I think then, possibly towards the end of the war my folks had an Eziot water heater put over the sink so that was the first time they had hot water in the house. And then... in 1957 they converted the back bedroom into a bathroom. They still didn't have an inside loo, the outside loo was there until they went. My dad used to go on a Sunday afternoon, put his scarf and his hat on and take the Sunday newspaper and go to the loo. A lot of people did it. Sometimes you had to shovel the blinking snow to get there.

Gas lights we had. In the middle of the room. There was a round ring... that used to catch all the black smoke, oh your rooms used to get filthy. There were two chains... on a piece of iron. You pulled it down to put it on and pulled the other one to put it off. You had a taper which you lit with a match and just held it up to it. It was a very poor light really. We always used to go to bed with a candle, we never used to bother lighting the upstairs one.

Front room was used at week-ends - week-ends, high days and holidays, Christmas, birthday if we had a party. What did we have? A sofa, two easy chairs, we had a side-board in there and an aspidistra... the biggest aspidistra in the world. They used to be ever so popular, I mean, nearly every house had one. They were ever so bushy. That's another thing you see, used to make your rooms dark, you'd got that bloody thing stuck in front of your window. And you used to have to feed it on cold tea.

We never had carpets anyway, all we had was the linoleum and a mat in the middle. In those days a rug it was like... by cutting old clothes up with the old peg through the sacking... pull them through the hole you'd made in the sack. That was one of the main things in the pawnbrokers, hanging outside. Cloth carpets but they were nice and warm in front of the fire.

The highlight of our week sometimes was on a Sunday night when we were all in... we'd push the table back and bring the... small armchairs from the front room and we'd all sit round and listen to the radio, I mean that was great, a super thing and the whole family sat there you know.

Twice a day... and sometimes three times

There were several places of worship in or near the area and, as these quotes show, many people's social lives revolved around their church or chapel.

As kids we all... mainly went to Holy Trinity church Sunday School... that's Regent Road. We didn't go to St Andrew's because I think we didn't like it. It was very high church and the vicar was Father Gilman, he wore a flowing cloak and he'd got a rather ugly face and he was quite a formidable character. A lot of people from that area went to Holy Trinity... or they went to the Methodist church. It was our social life.

Weren't allowed to have toys out on a Sunday. We could have books but we weren't allowed to have toys. We had to get dressed up and go out for a walk... in the morning with my dad while my mother got the dinner ready and then after tea we all used to go out for a walk, dressed up.

Sunday School outings - you went to Sunday School for a few weeks before that went you see, then you could go. I was with the Methodist in Crown Street then. You never went anywhere specific but you were in the country so you were out. We had the old charabanc, wooden seats, not coaches like they are now. You'd stop in this field and out would come the picnic baskets and you'd play games. If you found a hayrick you were in paradise.

St Andrew's Church
in 1995.
(C. Hyde)

The Jain Temple on
Oxford Street in
1995. This used to
be a Congregational
chapel.
(C. Hyde)

My parents went to, it was a Weslyan chapel on Aylestone Road but then they stopped going. I just used to go to Sunday School and special services at All Souls but then I did become quite involved at Oxford Street for quite a few years. Possibly because the boys were there that I liked... I was only twelve! It was a very big going concern. When I first went, and for quite a few years afterwards, for the anniversaries and the harvest festivals it would be choc-a-bloc downstairs and up in the balcony as well. But then of course it dwindled off over the years. We had a youth group going and we used to put on concerts and plays, I was in the choir as well. Apart from the youth group and the activities for the young people there were the men's clubs... whist drives, all sorts of activities for the older people as well.

I used to go to St Andrew's church in Jarrom Street. Well it was high church, it was incense. I joined the Church Lads Brigade while I was there. Father Gilman, he was there for quite a long while. He had a marvellous selection of butterflies and we always used to go in the vestry and he'd show us these. He were a great feller. He always used to come round the district and visit the elderly and he was very very popular I thought. It was well attended. We had the meetings... there were the band and there were practice. I played the bugle at a time. It was quite nice, we used to come down to St Andrew's in Knighton Street - church rooms - and do a bit of drilling... and then upstairs they'd got a little billiard table. It was just somewhere to go to pass a couple of nights away.

When we were little I used to have to go to Sunday School twice a day... on Sunday, and sometimes three times. I went to the Methodist church in Crown Street. I got named in All Souls because I didn't like St Andrew's, I didn't like the vicar Father Gilman. Horrible man, he was really. I was 19 when I got married - you don't want a sex talk and that's what he was doing, you must do this and you must do that, you know. St Andrew's was supposed to be Church of England but he changed it into Anglo Catholic. At 19 you don't want people telling you what to do what not to do anyway, but that sort of thing was very embarrassing in them days because we weren't so promiscuous as they are now, I mean nowadays well, they can tell you at 19 can't they, I mean I went red white and blue with embarrassment with him because he was... he didn't pull any punches and he was on about birth control and all this well you think, no I don't really want to know. Things like that weren't spoke about. You didn't talk about sex... say, 'I went out last night and, you know, did this', you wouldn't hear any talk like that, not even with the married women.

He was ever so nice (Father Gilman), he married me. He was a very nice person. The children used to take it out of him - I never did - 'cos his nose, it more or less went right out but that was done through... I think it was the First World War. We went to the vicarage once, I think it was when I went to put my banns in, and he'd got all these butterflies out, he'd got a lovely collection of butterflies... and he used to do all dried flowers and do all his own Christmas cards. If anybody needed help, such as forms signing or anything like that he'd go to their house and do it for them. He was a really good man.

One of my... it was my mother's mother's brother, very well made man... he was in the Salvation Army. They used to come on a regular basis and have their little service in Grasmere Street and then they would go from door to door with the collecting box and this uncle was the one with the collecting box. Grandma used to say, 'Oh it's Arthur again.' They had quite a thriving Sunday School as well for children. They used to parade round the streets... well they wouldn't actually parade but they'd just wander around, you know, how they do, and stop at various places, have a little service... knock on the door with a collecting box. They'd say, 'It's Uncle Arthur.'

Diphtheria

Although the Leicester Royal Infirmary was on the doorstep there was no GP in the area until recently. The nearest doctor's surgery was in Tower Street but there was a dispensary at the corner of Walnut Street and Aylestone Road.

If I was ill, which I was quite frequently, I always used to have a fire in the bedroom - they were the tiny little fireplaces and it was all coal fires. The first, worst one was even before I went to school... I had whooping cough and bronchial pneumonia which the doctor gave me up - he said it was only through mother's good nursing that brought me through. I went back to school, fortnight afterwards I was off with chicken pox, and then it would probably be when I was about seven I had diphtheria which I had to go to hospital with, and ten months afterwards I had scarlet fever. They did let me stay at home then because I was the only one, but I know the room... those days they said the room had to be 'stoved'. Mother had to keep a special gown or something to put on every time she came into the room and then when I was completely better someone had to come in... and disinfect it or what have you. I had everything else, measles, the lot, but they were the worst ones.

When I had the diphtheria there was quite an epidemic of it. I know when I was in hospital, the isolation ward at Groby Road, there were quite a few children died of it and I know when I had the scarlet fever there was an epidemic then. When I was in the hospital with the diphtheria your visitors couldn't come in the ward to see you, you spoke to them through a glass window. It was very grim.

There was an old fashioned way of every Friday night it was the syrup of figs - yeah, horrible. On the other side of it, because I suppose I was such a little weakling I was given Virol and cod liver oil to build me up.

Did you hear about the diphtheria epidemic? It started, now let me see... 1923, just before I sat my first examination at school. I can remember having a pain in my throat. The doctor came and took a swab and you took that to the education place in Carts Lane. Course when you're admitted they give you all the treatment, put acid on your hair, 'cos I mean lice was rife in those days you know. It started in that area. I was six weeks in hospital and then you had a month prior to going back to school and I went back to school, had a week, and they closed... Hazel Street school down for a month.

South of Walnut Street in 1968, showing the sports grounds, the power station, the canal, the cattle market and the allotments. *(Leicester Mercury)*

LEISURE

Street life

The Walnut Street area of the past was a much safer and better place for children to play. There were more play areas available, as well as the open spaces of the allotments on Freemen's Common. The absence of cars meant that the streets, with all their alleyways and courtyards, were a playground too.

Street life? Enjoyable. Marbles, fag cards, run races, whip and top was great - that was on pancake day wasn't it? Another favourite with us, we'd call it 'gratering.' Now underneath quite a few of the houses round there, not all of them, was a cellar where the coal was kept. There was a square iron cover which, when the coal man arrived, you'd go down the cellar and unhook it. And at the side of it was a grating... to enable light to get into the cellar. Anyone walking by, they might drop a marble down there. If the sun shone you might find a penny but of course the grate was that depth down so we had a cane... if you were found or seen gratering... the man or the lady of the house might come out, say, 'Clear off,' then they'd go and have a look for what it was you were looking for.

We used to have a cane split with a matchstick in the bottom to hold it open... with a bit of chewing gum on the end. We were just allowed to go, we had to be in by a certain time but, no, when I look back it was just total freedom and nobody was worried. I mean I wouldn't have done it with my kids.

You'd have a job to play football in the street. Nobody, even your own parents wouldn't allow you to play football in the street. Some of the old dears, if you happened to get near them they'd tell you to go in front of your own windows, 'cos I mean there were the tops, some of them were called window breakers weren't they?

We used to make our own fun really, playing football in the street... we made a ball up from newspaper, used to wet the newspaper, rag and string, and tie it. Then it came to the India rubber balls, people did have those. It was frowned on really but we used to do it because we didn't want to go up to Welford Road recce. All cobbled and we used to play... one manhole to there was that goal and the other goal was that manhole to that one. About half a dozen of us played.

Granby Halls

That was never called Granby Halls, that was called the Junior Training Halls and from what I was told it was more or less training the territorials in World War One. At the Granby Halls there there used to be a big horse trough in the centre. There was just horses and carts and people riding bikes. I mean, you just walked across. There were nothing to dodge out of the way of, I mean you could run faster than horse and cart. The trams were there, they were very good. They always used to go to the Aylestone tram terminus from The Bedford. Only trouble is when you'd got the bikes, you got in the tramlines and you got thrown off.

We used to spend an awful lot of time going up to Western Park, 'cos we used to be able to go up there for a ha'penny return. Tram used to stop outside the park. Braunstone Gate... there's this big iron bridge, that's where you used to catch the tram, used to take you right up to the park. Without Mum - be about six, seven. You could go out, you weren't afraid of being took off by somebody like they are now.

There used to be a lot of kids on this street. I mean, at least 20 I should think, at least... on just our part of the street. There was a lot of children. I should say a good third of the houses now are student houses. The parents used to take it in turns... up 'til you were about six or seven, you'd go on your own then.

Just a few houses away... there were another group of children who were a few years older and I remember my mother saying to one of the older girls she would let me go out to play if she'd look after me. And I think this is what happened, the older ones tended to keep an eye on the little ones.

Don't forget... there wasn't the cars and that about. I mean nearly everything then was horse drawn, the milkman, the baker, the coalman, the deliveries that you see being made to factories. The rag and bone man came round once a week with his horse and cart. I used to hate it 'cos we had... quite a big garden at the back then and I used to have to go out with my bucket and dustpan.

We were certainly allowed to wander around - much more so than you'd dare allow a child to wander these days.

Youth clubs, recce's and the Regal

As well as a number of youth clubs, there were three parks, or recreation grounds (recce's), in the immediate area - Welford Road, Thirlmere Gardens, and Filbert Street. The Regal cinema was built on Havelock Street in the 1930s and closed in 1959. Although the building is still there, it is now used by an electrical wholesaler.

We went pictures, we were always at pictures. If we weren't at pictures we went to the youth centre which was at Hazel Street school. And one of the blokes who used to come and teach us at Hazel Street was Don Revie - you know Don Revie the footballer? - well he used to come there, he came when he broke his leg. They're just supposed to be doing something like that now but it's old hat that was really. That was our youth centre. Before then... we had a youth centre in... it was a big cellar on the grounds of Freeman Hardy and Willis. Lewis I think his name was. We had to do it up, we'd got it on the thing that we decorated it out, you know. We had woodworking and table-tennis, 'cos you didn't have things like you've got today. But then when we went to Hazel Street, Hazel Street were fitted out really, you know, a big hall upstairs, playing five-a-side football. My father went to that school.

There was nothing to do unless you belonged to something like a church youth club, but there were the boys clubs as well which I had nothing to do with. There was never any buzz in Leicester at any time that I can recall, it was always known as a bit of a dead city... everything died at half past ten.

They started a bit of a youth club round at St Andrew's church... I think Hazel Street used to have a youth club as well. PT weren't it, some of the boys'd do, and bit of woodwork... modelling with clay... I mean I took some lovely ashtrays home to my mum - got put in the bin but I thought they were alright. It won't sound exciting to you but to them in those days it was terribly exciting to be out of sight of their mums and dads and, you know, they could do what they wanted and it didn't matter.

Just in round the corner from Aylestone Street... there used to be the old St Andrew's church rooms... and I remember Father Gilman... from St Andrew's church used to run the scouts and things and they seemed to frizzle a bit as time went on but I was in the cubs. My mother and father couldn't afford a uniform for me either. There was quite a lot of lads in the cubs and they came from a wide area.

City players Joe Calvert, Don Revie (the future England manager), and Mal Griffiths sign a young fan's autograph book in 1947. (Leicester Evening Mail)

There was a roller skating rink on the Boulevard but I never went myself. We used to play on the Welford Road recreation ground but it were never in any condition it is now, I mean the grass'd be about that high... it was, you could never see your football and that.

We did enjoy that little park (Thirlmere). It was all grass, there was the pavilion in the centre where the elderly people used to sit. There was a park keeper who kept a very strict eye on you, you weren't allowed to race around there because of disturbing people who were sitting and resting. But there was this little boating pond there and... it was quite wide on the edge, you could sort of sit on it or walk on it and I remember taking my cousin on there once and he fell in. People were always falling in - you could often see the children running out of the gate dripping wet, crying. It was a very nice little park.

Well they, they always used to be allotments. That was before World War One, that was just a triangle of allotments.

And all around it was wooden trestles with all roses on, I mean you couldn't take a ball on there when I were a lad, if he caught you with a ball, the park keeper, 'Be off!' All the flower beds round the side and the hedges were all trimmed, all the privet hedges went up and down like that all the way.

Where the football ground car park is now, that used to be a recreation ground with swings and everything on it.

There was small toilets there... there was a square positioned off and nobody walked on that, and that was a cricket pitch and people say, 'I can't believe that', because they'd be hitting the ball

The Regal Cinema.
The building is still on
Havelock Street.
(Leicester Mercury)

in the canal but they never did. It was a biggish place. You'd got the children's play area there, the swings.

At the top of Filbert Street you get onto the recce climbing over the railings and that went along by the canal to what we knew as Parsons Field and that was, eventually they used that for the power station. You'd got to go down there by five o'clock to get a place to play. Then again... you were lucky to have a ball 'cos nobody had a ball in those days. Piece of rag tied up with string, that was our ball, or go to the slaughterhouse. Used to stand there and wait for a pig's bladder. Just blow it up and tie it off, they were strong. If we wanted a bat... one of the groundsmen down the County... you might get a broken one, then you saw the end off. You daren't play in the street, only on the recce.
That was on the recreation ground they kept sheep. All recce's. How I know is, I went to school with Frank Clark, his father was a sheep farmer and he lived in Brazil Street. Through the old iron gates down to the recce, gates at the bottom to keep the sheep in. The chief job the old groundsman did was clean the sheep droppings off the centre pitch, put 'em on the back of his shed and the gardeners from the commons would pay him a tanner (2p) a bag for it.

There were some swings all over there where the football ground car park is now and also there were air-raid shelters there. There were some air-raid shelters went underground, two or three there at the end of the war. We were allowed to play around on there. I think after the war they filled them air-raid shelters in. This end of the stand were all burnt down... same as the top end of the Rugby stand were burnt down at the Tigers - we used to play underneath this end here - there used to be all ammunition boxes in there, we used to climb on top of them. About the end of the war.

(In the 1920s), we played in Sawday Street between the factories. It was only factories down there. I can remember all them being allotments. When I was a little lad I remember going to the infants school in Sawday Street, which is Hazel Street infants. There was only one other building and that was the games room for the All Souls church, that was on its own.

Victoria Park, we went to Abbey Park - we used to take our children. We'd walk along the canal to Abbey Park, no problem as we got older, not when we were little obviously. We used to bike for miles - Abbey Park, Bradgate Park, Groby Pool. We've walked from Bradgate Park before now. The children of today are going to lose the use of their legs - they are even taken to the school...

To go the pictures we'd go to the Regal, we never went into the town. We waited for the film to come from town to the Regal.

That used to be Lewitts the boot and shoe factory and there was a fire there. We woke to see that fire. I can remember that because my brother and I, we both got up and we came down and we were forced back... we got into Winifred Street and the block, the building there, the wall collapsed and it came straight across the road into Winifred Street. Course we thoroughly enjoyed that, it were great. Then the cinema was after that.

The Regal, Olympia... Roxy. Olympia was over the Narborough Road bridge. When we were courting my brother would go to the Regal... and then he'd come in and he'd sit, and you don't want little boys round do you when you're courting and I said to him, 'Do you want to go to the Olympia?' I'd give him ten pence and he'd shoot over the bridge and go to the pictures, second half and all, just to get him out of the way. The Regal was very popular. You'd go out Sunday afternoon and you used to go to the museum... to get a date for Sunday night down the Regal didn't you. And it used to be seven pence, nine pence and one and six (7p) in the balcony. Course as you got older you started going into town pictures didn't you, they were all over, there were so many cinemas in town.

At the Regal cinema I've stood outside there many an hour when there was 'A' films. When I were about twelve, thirteen. Used to wait out there, you'd ask someone to take you in, you know, a grown-up person. Sometimes after you'd been there a while the manager used to say, 'Alright you two can go in.'

Out in the open

Not only could you once go swimming in the canal, but warm water from the power station meant that the fishing was good as well. There were allotments stretching from what is now Southfields College up to Freemen's Common. Nearby was the Cattle Market, which closed in the late 1980s and is awaiting redevelopment.

I used to go swimming on the Bede House - Walnut Street bridge, well just on the canal... a big area which was the old Bede House. Only cost you a penny, take your own costume and towel and swim in the canal. It used to be crowded in the summer... crowded. A few years went by and then they put boards on the bridges, 'This water is unsuitable for swimming'. It dropped off. I knew a fellow when I was 14, he used to go down for a swim at the Bede House every morning before he went to work. It used to be crowded, hundreds of kiddies... I used to dive off the bridge.

I've been going down to the Working Men's Club... that started in Clarendon Street that did. It used to be, when I was a lad, you couldn't get in the place at the weekend, they used to have concerts every weekend. There used to be three turns on... a comedian, a singer, either someone like a ventriloquist or someone tap-dancing. Each turn used to do about ten minutes and then another one. It used to be packed. There used to be no end of club turns around in Leicester. The younger people, they're all for these nightclubs now aren't they?

The canal, they've let that go. I mean we used to swim down there when I were a kid. It was clear, there were no weeds in it. What we used to do, you know how you are when you're kids - when the barges used to bring coal and stuff - you'd got to swim and dive under it and swim under it. You know, for a dare. It were a greeny colour the water was. From the Bede House, we used to sit outside... in the hot weather just all sunbathing, swimming, then we'd run along here, get on this bridge and jump off.

I can remember one lad - we used to do it, at the side of the bridge we ran down the slope and dived in and he got caught in one of the old dustbin things. We had to get him out and rush him up to the Infirmary. It were filthy in fact. Afterwards there was notices up to say swimming not allowed.

Then there was the canal... fishing along the canal with a pole and a bent pin catching gudgeon. There's hardly any fish in there now.

My father had an allotment. You know where the Bede House is, the bridge and just along there, it used to be all allotments... we'd got a den and that. Freemen's Common, terrific... we hadn't got gardens so you'd got to grow your own vegetables because it was cheaper and it was better for you anyway. There were some little cottages top end of Freemen's Common. We used to spend... hours up there train spotting. Wild strawberries grew up there, we were well away in the strawberry season. And in the winter it was great for sledging down that hill. I'd pack some sandwiches, some pop and a flask of tea, go up, and we'd perhaps sit there 'til eight o'clock at night in the summer.

Up the side of the Tiger's ground we used to call it the Black Pad, it was the Tiger's ground on one side and allotments on the other side. That was just before you came to the cattle market.

Course then you see you had Freemen's Common as well, did you hear about that? All the old houses up there with no electricity in them and people used to live in there. They used to call that pub there... there's a pub up there, years ago they used to call it the longest bar in Leicester... 'cos they always used to go down the pub, buy the booze, and go back to their places and sit outside drinking it. The allotments were the thing in them days as well weren't they, everybody went on the allotments. We used to go up and sit there, a little hut, and make a cup of tea, sitting with the runner beans and that.

Wholesale meat... we used to go down there and stock up with meat... half the price you'd get from the butcher. At Christmas time we used to go up the cattle market and bid for our chickens... and your eggs and everything. That used to be an outing for the children, Wednesdays, take them up the cattle market, see all the animals, that was the nearest they got to animals.

Before Berrys (the scrapyard) went there, used to be at the foot of Western Boulevard there's access to the railway, that used to be the Great Central cattle docks. When they used to bring them along that line they just drove them out and up into the abattoirs, and they come down our way you see along Grasmere Street. Many a time - I don't know if you know but if a cow sees an empty, it'll go - times they've been down the entries along Grasmere Street. You forget these things don't you? I used to live up there, that were my second home. And the market policeman were called Dobney... and he'd got this cane - cor, you didn't let him see you - swish! They used to have a market on Saturday as well as Wednesday. Used to go every Wednesday 'cos you get to know these farmers and they used to have free range eggs you see.

Used to spend no end of time up the cattle market watching them slaughtering the cows in the old slaughter houses. Course they used to be ever so busy then. There was a smell, I mean, 'cos... all the intestines. Pull them in out of the pen on a rope through this hole in the window and then put it round a bar like and hold 'em there. Used to shoot 'em in the head, I think it were what they called a bolt. After they fell on the floor they used to put a thin like bamboo cane down and they used to kick like buggery - tickling their brain or something. Then they used to haul them up on pull-blocks. They'd cut their throat and drain all the blood out and then they'd sort of saw them in half, well, skin them first... cut the things out, all the intestines, then cut them in two halves, then when they'd washed them down they'd push them out on these... hooks like. You could still see the meat moving when it were in the halves like, you know, nerves still moving. Oh yeah, we used to spend no end of times up there.

Blue Army!

Local memories of Leicester City stretch back to the 1920s.

Everybody were coming down on their bikes. The houses in Filbert Street, Hazel Street, and Grasmere Street, they used to store their bikes for about tuppence or threepence.

We had got a yard... and they used to bring their bikes in and leave their bikes there for sixpence, two or three of them. Mum gave it to me and my sister like - we thought it was great. 'Cos there was nowhere to park them down Filbert Street.

We used to store bikes in the yard for down the City. I've had as many as 50 bikes in the yard. Course they used to get gates of 40,000 then. That was in the days of John Duncan, he was the captain.

Mother and Father, they were very big supporters of the Tigers... so we had to more or less be members there but there were times when I used to - when mother were getting tea ready - used to change and I used to run down to Filbert Street and watch the last ten minutes. You could always get in then free, they always opened the gates about ten minutes before. The back windows of Grasmere Street, which is now Burnmoor Street, well there were no sheds there and the old ladies... well there were open doors, they could go in there and go into the back bedroom and see the match there,

Floodlights being erected at Filbert Street in 1957
(Leicester Mercury)

overlooking the football pitch. Supporters perhaps give 'em a copper or two, they had a cup of tea, and they had a good view for nothing really.

I always remember Arthur Chandler, he said... he'd broken more windows in Filbert Street than any kid. Put two goals in the net... if the others go over the top, well that's a bit of bad luck for the people living in Filbert Street.

I used to stand in my bedroom (in Filbert Street), when I were a young lad, I could see about three quarters of the pitch and watch it from my bedroom window 'til they built this Captain's Table.

The only time I saw... I was really frightened. I used to go football, thought it was great... Nottingham Forest were coming to play (in the 1960s), and they were saying there was going to be trouble - they'd just knocked down Clarendon Street and Raglan Street so it's going back a bit - so my dad says, 'No there's not.' So I says, 'Well I'm not stopping, there's going to be trouble.' But I went to see my Auntie Pat... as I came out there's this huge mob coming down New Bridge Street, right across the road they were, and they were picking sticks and bricks up off the debris that was... well, I ran up my mum's entry and I said, 'I'm going, I'm not stopping here, there's going to be trouble.' And there was trouble 'cos all the shop windows got broken didn't they, and that's the first time I ever remember any vandalism down there. It was a shock to us who lived there because we'd never had anything like that.

Pubs

There were around 24 pubs in the area at one time.

There was more pubs than anything down that area you know. The one next to me (The Rifle Butts) they had what you don't see nowadays, you used to be able to go in the front door... and they had what used to call a 'Bobby Hole' and the old dears used to go with their jugs and they'd sit and have half a glass of beer and then come out with their jug of beer and go home.

I remember my mum and dad sending me down to Walnut Street, there was an off licence, and I'm talking what, seven, eight. And I always had a sip of beer coming home.

That's what you don't hear now in pubs... you never hear a sing song going on. Yet in the summer you could hear, all the doors and the windows were open and you'd hear them all singing. Let's face it the songs they play now you can't sing anyway. My mum and dad... always used to go in The Nags Head and Star in Oxford Street. My mum... she would be making sandwiches, she would be doing mussels and they'd take a jar and vinegar and they'd have a picnic more or less in the pub, and then they'd start - the songs would go up. I mean... if we'd been out, my boyfriend and I, we'd try and end up back there for the last half hour 'cos you could guarantee there'd be a right good sing song and then we'd wander down here on our own, still singing... you know, unless anything went wrong and then there'd be a row.

That's where the social life was, see, we didn't have television and things, that's where everything used to go off, in the pub. Course different pubs had different landlords and all had their different ways didn't they and most of them were money lenders. Blokes like George Fisher'd

The Gladstone pub was at the corner of Raglan Street and Havelock Street. *(M & J Zientek)*

lend money out to people. They'd got it. I remember he lent some money to a chap during the war, he were telling me, and he turned out to be a trainer for Lord Rothschild the horse racer. George lent him... 30 bob (£1.50) for bed and breakfast, and of course George never thought he'd see it again, you know, and this bloke, after the war, came and found him - he lived in France at this big chateau - and I've seen cheques for thousands of pounds have gone over in horse racing tips. Fishers were very nice people, they were very good to us. We'd got nothing, I mean we had no coke at one time, it were very cold and George fetched some of the big coke up from the boiler and tipped it down the cellar for me. We all helped each other didn't we, we had to, we were all in the same boat more or less.

Escaping elephants and other stories

Old men chewed the road and elephants roamed the street!

I know one year, I would be about seven at the time, used to have the circus come to Granby Halls and this particular year - they always used to put them in the stables over the road in one of the public house stables - but this particular year they'd set up a business so they couldn't do it and they didn't know where they could put the animals, so they finished up down in our stables, a big elephant and a baby elephant and four camels in the garage. And I remember that the trainer of the elephants, he used to have the big elephant chained and it would go through the hayloft... and he would sleep up in the hayloft. He'd got some relatives a little way away and he wanted to visit them, so he did. My brother... said he'd look after the whatsit (elephant), well he'd come in for a meal and the elephant managed to get out, lift the bar of the big gates... he'd got out and he was looking in the window of the shop opposite which was Paynters, three balls, pawn shop, when somebody came running in, 'The elephant's out, the elephant's out!' My brother went and got it back and stayed with it. That was a real laugh that was.

Bonfire night, you'd go round there (Pentonville), magnificent bonfire... 1925-ish. The police'd be round because the fire was dangerous, I mean, it's only narrow, and there's this whacking great bonfire in the middle. The boys and girls realised, so the police'd come round and have a look -

you'd actually see him. There wasn't a scrap of rubbish anywhere. When he'd gone everybody'd bring all their rubbish out - there's the bonfire again.

Bonfire nights always used to fascinate me because there always used to be the big bonfire on the recce - Welford Road recce - there used to be a bonfire somewhere near Kentish Street... they used to have bonfires in the street, in the middle of the road as well. Some were cobbled, Aylestone Street wasn't. There were the odd street parties... everyone had flags and put bunting across the street for the Coronation. All the mothers and fathers were allowed to go to the Regal cinema to watch the Coronation... I never saw it.

When did the King come to the throne - King George? '36 I thought it was. We'd got all these lights all - we was in Victoria Street - all outside the window, and we had a big party down the bottom. It chucked it down with rain during the night and fused all the lights.

Thirlmere Street and Windemere Street used to have cobbled roads and the tar was all in the middle and we used to go out when it was hot with a stick - a little matchstick or something - and wind it on and roll it into a ball, this tar. Put it on your bedside table and it stopped you having headaches. Some of the old men used to get it and they used to chew it... just like chewing gum, they never swallowed it... and believe it or not they swore by it for their teeth.

The only pub we used to go in was The Bedford, facing Granby Halls, which is not called The Bedford anymore now is it - The Victory that's it. Used to go in there because my pal's dad used to keep that one, Evans his name was. We used to hold our - I was in a scooter club when I was 16, you know, Lambrettas - and we used to hold the scooter club meetings first there and then later on across the other one on the opposite corner.

It was a very friendly area actually. We used to be into racing and all sorts, you know, noisy exhaust systems and very anti-social, and I remember one lady at the top of the street telling my mum that she always used to know what time of night it was by hearing my scooter coming down the road, and my mum used to say she used to know when I was on my way home about 15 minutes before I got there. Things that you'd frown upon now isn't it?

I do remember just one person ever complaining and that was the house that lived directly opposite because obviously they were... little entries between the houses and I used to keep my scooter in the backyard in a shed. I used to ride it down the entry under power, you know, rather than push it, and this one opposite used to reckon it made his windows rattle and he came out and complained one night, gave me a bit of abuse - he's the only one I ever remember. They certainly never thought of going to the local authority and complaining about something, it was always... have a word with your parents or have a word with you, but not so much on the quiet word in your ear basis as the yelling and screaming basis.

The Agricultural Show

I can remember when we had the agricultural show. About six or seven o'clock in the morning we used to go along Aylestone Road to where the show was which is now the electricity, Raw Dykes Road, and we used to go there and get free milk because they milked the cows before the show. And the show was more or less, the big marquees were on the county cricket ground... and then where... the electricity is and Raw Dykes, that were the rest of the show. And we used to walk home with the free milk. Mother used to get a kind of muslin and just strain it and that's it.

SCHOOL DAYS

Many people's education was very similar: learn the three Rs until the age of 14 and then find a job. Few people went into higher education, often because their families needed an extra income. Also, attitudes were different: one man remembers that when he decided to become a surveyor the local gossip was that he was going beyond his station.

Dancing round the Maypole at Hazel Street School. *(Hazel Street School)*

Walking to school we used to walk past... a big iron foundry and that was always fascinating. We used to stare through the windows at all sorts of exciting things going on in there. I remember that being an absolutely horrible place, really black and dirty, and these strange, like coal miner looking people scuttling around inside. It really was hell in there looking through the windows. There's a little cut through there we used to walk through... that was our route to school.

You went up Joseph Street and that, there was a foundry there. I can remember one of the furnaces was Joseph Street side because I mean you could feel the heat in the wall from there. Children used to stand there, really warm.

Certainly the kids that were further up by the hospital off New Bridge Street, from Havelock upwards, generally were not considered to be quite clean or not awfully well dressed. You saw it in the way the kids were at school, in the way they were dressed and the way they were sent out. And the teachers showed it in favouritism to them, I mean I know I was a teacher's favourite... because my mother sent me out clean and tidy and well dressed - we hadn't got a lot of money but...

You could tell by the way they dressed but nobody seemed to really worry about that, there were no class distinction or anything like that.

Junior schools

As well as Hazel Street School, St Andrew's church had schools in Laxton Street and Deacon Street until the 1950s.

When I was at junior school there was definitely two quite strong gangs and one was led by a blonde good looking girl and she was a right tough nut. I can remember us having gang fights in New Bridge Street when I was well under ten. We had some quite good punch ups.

Hazel Street. First of all you'd got the infants which was Sawday Street. I have recollections of that and of having naps in these folding beds in the afternoon in the playground... and dancing the Maypole. I've got a picture of me dancing the Maypole in a little silk suit with buttons and bows. In 1939 that was, I was going up to Hazel Street which was the junior school and of course that was the outbreak of war. Because of the outbreak of war they were strengthening the buildings so we actually for half a year only went to school half-time - half the school went in the morning, half in the afternoon.

It was a typical Board School, split into two, boys and girls, and the two didn't mix. The headmaster was Pop Vial and he was the most gorgeous man I ever met in my life. White haired man. He was super to the people he liked but he was a sod to people he didn't like and... a group of kids used to come from Countesthorpe homes... and I can remember seeing him beat these kids, he was quite nasty with them. It was quite strange really. He had a very different attitude from the people he liked.

We had air-raid practice. I can remember having to go out in the yard with our gas masks and there was supposed to be mustard gas in the middle of the playground and according to the direction of the wind you were supposed to go round away from the thing.

There was another teacher there called Mrs Humphries and Mrs Humphries always had her favourites. I remember she took us to her house on a number of occasions, we went for tea. She lived in a very posh house in Kings Mead Road, Knighton. It was quite a treat actually, wonderful back garden, bathroom and everything.

I went to Laxton Street School and then I went to Deacon Street, the other one, they were both St Andrew's schools. Got my eleven plus from there and went to the Alderman Newton's. It (Laxton Street) was up to seven year olds and then after that you went to Deacon Street. It was a nice big yard as I remember it, and you had to go in in Gosling Street... but there was a main rather posh door in Laxton Street, more like a church door. We used to go... St Andrew's Day we all had to march to church to a service and then we had the rest of the day off.

Deacon Street, I went to school in that area, it was called St Andrew's School. That was the infants, from three upwards. It was a very very small school, only perhaps about four rooms in it - one big hall - then three little rooms. They used to put you to sleep on little fold up beds in the afternoon in the big hall when you was in the... nursery. You used to have symbols... I was always

The Open Air School

I was very ill, I had asthma and the doctor kept me off school. There was a special school at Western Park, we used to call it the open air school and it took me about a year to get in there and I never went back to Hazel Street school. I used to catch a tram from Braunstone Gate that took you up to the Western Park gates. If you lived a long way away... they used to give you special tickets to get free tram passes. You used to take all your coats off and they used to give you like a, you know these polo neck goalkeepers, like the goalkeepers used to wear, used to wear one of them like. If it was bitter cold you used to have the classrooms with big glass windows and they used to have them wide open and it used to be perished. All they had behind the teacher at the front, they had a coke fire, one of them brazier things. After dinner you used to have what they called an hour's rest and they used to have these canvas beds and a wooden frame and, you know, in the summer there was a big grass lawn, a big asphalt playing area, and they used to lay your beds out in rows... and in the winter you'd lay out there if it was dry. No matter how cold it were you just lay there with just one blanket on. You'd freeze. That was for asthma, that's how they used to treat you. I used to come home at night from there and I couldn't hardly turn the key in the back door 'cos my hands were so cold.

the purse. Where you put your shoes it was like a big piece of hessian with all these symbols embroidered on it, and you were either a windmill, flower, or purse, something like that. There wasn't a lot of children in the school. On your bed you had this symbol, on your milk thing.

Secondary school and after

Some pupils attended Gateway School, but others had to travel outside the area.

When we went for our examinations when we were eleven and twelve we went to Queen's Road... Clarendon Park is it? You got a piece of cardboard, a new rule, pen and pencil, and we all walked up there, had the examination there and all walked back. If you got a scholarship you went free to the grammar school - Alderman Newton's, Wyggeston and that - but if you got a second class your parents had to pay so much, and if you got a third class you could go to the intermediate school which was King Richard's Road.

I passed my eleven plus, quite high mark, and Wyggeston Girls' was the school to go... it was like the cream, and I put down on my choice of schools, Wyggeston Girls', Alderman Newton's... well I didn't get in Wyggeston Girls', I got in the Alderman Newton. I think it was two or three years later... I found out I'd got the academic qualifications for Wyggeston but because I lived in York Road I wasn't... it was classed as a poor area, I couldn't afford to go to Wyggeston Girls'. They kind of only had people from Evington, Highfields - if you lived at Highfields you were rich. I think it's because socially Wyggeston Girls' was very... the upper class people. I mean, there was that class distinction in those days (1950s).

The Gateway School at that time (1940s) was an experimental school. It was one of the first... it was a technical secondary school, it gave people a technical biased education. It also allowed people to come in who didn't get their scholarship or, later on, their eleven plus, if they took another exam when they were thirteen. They'd got a whole section for builders, they'd got engineers, people doing boot and shoe, and hosiery. It was very allied to the Technical College, we did a lot of our technical work over in the college itself. I consider it was a very very good school. It was never considered a snobbish school whereas the Wyggeston was the snobs school as we saw it.

Gateway School from 1959. We used the chapel on Oxford Street, it's the temple now I think. Every morning the whole school used to leave Gateway, walk down Bonners Lane, turn left by Morleys and then walk across the road - held all the traffic up - for school service, then they marched us all back again.

In those days there wasn't the emphasis put on education as there is now. There was the College of Art and Technology... but I don't think I ever knew anyone who went there even if it was on the doorstep, that was something that tended to come after you'd started to work when people were starting to get more education conscious.
I don't think many people from the New Bridge Street area from my time actually were that worried about doing any further education. Most people lived in the area... a hell of a lot of them used to work for Bentleys engineering, there were one or two other engineering firms, and hosiery

firms, Swanns, there was a foundry. That was in Joseph Street. There was the... a bottle factory of some sort. The Liberty was there, Attenboroughs, Russells, they were all sort of hosiery factories.

I wanted to work in a shop actually. The headmaster at King Richard's Road was quite upset... he wanted me to stay on to take what was then known as a matriculation exam 'cos he said I ought to work in a bank or somewhere like that. You see... my dad hadn't got a particularly highly paid job and he wanted me at work earning money. He said he couldn't afford for me to stay on at school. I went to the Co-op. That was my first choice and I got on.

When I was in my last year (1940s) at school and I decided I was going to be a surveyor, certainly there were things said in the street, you know, that I was going above my station, I can tell you that because it got back to my folks and got back to me through a friend's parents that people were saying, 'Well he's going well above his station.' It's strange isn't it, they saw you had a station in life and you didn't try and climb out of it.

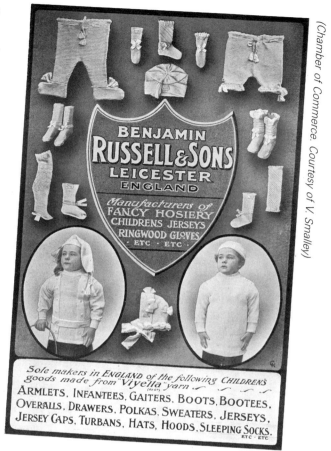

(Chamber of Commerce. Courtesy of V. Smalley.)

Bloody kids!

As everyone knows, when kids today misbehave it is vandalism, but when they acted up in the past it was just a bit of harmless fun! These quotes show that children haven't changed over the years.

As a kid... we had used to go and pinch bottles of pop out of this greengrocer's shop in Aylestone Street. He used to keep all his stock in the entry and it was never ever locked. There used to be some allotments - Freemen's Common - and we used to go scrumping there, pinching flowers, and there was a strawberry bank... it's part of the railway embankment on the Freemen's Common and in the summer there used to be all these strawberries. You could get into the cattle market... climb over the walls at night. I remember a regular trick we used to do as kids. The Salvation Army in Jarrom Street... they used to have their prayer evenings... we used to go and collect all the empty milk bottles that people had put out and we used to put them outside the

Sally Army's door because the doors used to open out and we used to hammer on the door and they used to come and undo these doors and break all these milk bottles. I'd have got a hell of a good hiding if my mother and father had ever found out.

(In the 1920s) the bottom of Mill Lane on the embankment there used to be gorse bushes. They used to set fire to the bushes and then call for the fire brigade, then run down to see them put it out.

I used to be in the Girl Guides and all I did... St Andrew's church hall. We used to go out Broughton Astley. Then as we got older we put our Guides' uniforms on and go and meet the boys and say we'd been to Guides. Mum never did know. The favourite one was tying a bit of cotton onto a letter box and threading it all up the street and pulling all the letter boxes. Daft, but it was fun. The people just used to ignore it if the letter boxes went... you'd just say, 'The bloody kids are tying cotton round the letter boxes again.' 'Cos you knew what time the postman came.

The old lady at number 42, she were a devil, she really was, she lived on her own. You'd only got to walk past her front and she'd more or less clear you off. So she often got her letter box rapped. I used to get on with her alright really. In order to earn a bit of money you used to do errands and there were three ladies in the street I had to go to every night from school. I didn't necessarily have any errands to do but I had to see if they wanted any. They asked my mother if I could you see. I got sixpence a week.

Houses with cellars which were substantial and, if you had a lot of children, that was used as a punishment block, you put the children in the cellar.

My father, living near the Commons, he said to me, 'If ever I know you to go scrumping you won't be able to lay down on your bed for a week.' And I never went scrumping.

The making-up room at A.W. Swann & Co. Ltd in 1968. *(Leicester Mercury)*

WALNUT STREET AT WORK

Is the job regular?

The Walnut Street area had a great variety of industry. There were hosiery factories, boot and shoe factories, dye works, engineering firms, and many others. Famous names included Liberty, Bentleys, Stibbes, and Armstrong Siddeley. However, in the 1920s and 1930s the country was in a depression and work was scarce. Although Leicester suffered less than most other cities, many working class people felt the pinch.

Unemployment? Deep memories. My own father round about 1931... good job, hosiery trimmer, and like as today, depression. Then of course, which I do recall, we had people come to the house... it was called, or nick-named, the means test... I do know at home the piano was taken. It was ours, the piano, my mother's dressing tables which were two beautiful things and quite a few other things that were taken and sold, right, before you got any money from the government. He was unemployed as far as I can recall for about eight years. Mother'd do cleaning, anything to make ends meet. I went to work at 15. I took on a paper round during this means test period at two and six (12p) a week, that's early morning and it wasn't for a long long time afterwards that I found that the means test were taking something like two shilling (10p) out of the two and six. They deducted it from what my mum and dad were receiving. I knew very little about that.

In those days you know... they didn't ask you how much you got, they said is the job regular? To get a regular job you were very lucky. You were brought up to economise everywhere. She would never go in debt, she'd never go down the pawnshop - that was one of the lowest you can get, going down the pawnshop.

We weren't a poor household. I do remember, it would be in the 1930s... I know lots and lots of people were off work and my father was on short time and my mother then had work out. Quite a few years ago just before my mother died she lent me a locket... she said, 'I haven't got a chain to go with it... I did have a chain years ago but when your father was on short time I sold it to help ends meet and your father sold his gold guard as well.' I honestly think, looking back, that I was well clothed and I think it was my mother went without. I think this was it, being the only one I was spoilt.

After my mum decided she didn't want to do fish and chips any longer the shop opened as a hosiery shop. When I was getting a bit older... he'd (Dad) do the winding and the wool and he'd got ladies that'd got Griswold machines and we used to take the bobbins of yarn... down to these different places, different houses, where the ladies did the socks and that, and then we'd have to go and fetch them back when they'd done them, take them somewhere else so the ladies could toe them... and then we'd have to take them down to... at the corner of Jarrom Street and Asylum Street... there was a factory where they pressed them. And then my dad had to have them back, put them into boards, do them up, and he was doing them for a school somewhere down south...

Oxford way. He did that for years. He did others, he did just ordinary socks. My mother then... she'd meet me after school and we'd go over to Coalville, miners' socks, we had a stall over there.

At Russells. Then, my aunty worked there and they asked her to come and tell me that they wanted someone for overlocking. Would I like to go and learn? So I went and they taught me. I'd been used to big premises and as I knew one or two of the people who worked there it was quite alright. It wasn't all that noisy or smelly.

I left when I was 14 (in 1927), went and got me own job... Wildt, Wildt Mellor Bromley, well it was Wildt's then, his father was a German. Top of Filbert Street... a hosiery factory have got it now, it's changed two or three times. Not all that big, about 30, 40 people. First day clean the office plate outside. I remember one of my jobs was fetching milk from the shop for the girls. I got a home made tray full of cups of milk... and I were walking along Coniston Avenue and the kids had just come off the - louts they were - and they emptied half my tray drinking this milk and I couldn't do anything about it. I always remember that.

I finished at Narborough Road when I was 14 and from there I went - 'cos you could go and find your own jobs then or your mother took you - I went and got a job in a shoe factory on the Boulevard and my mother said, 'You're not going... I've been in boot and shoes and it's very hard work.' My mother used to sit up all hours of the night working on shoes and that, you know, and sewing buttons on and all that sort of thing just for some money... to keep the house going, and my father was at work. As I say, there wasn't a lot of money about in them days in any job. I finished up at Russells... down on the Boulevard. On every floor they did different things, babywear on one floor, jumpers on another, that sort of thing. I went in the boxing department, Mr Burgess, I used to put labels on boxes. You used to do about a 48 hour week... I used to get ten shilling (50p) for that.

A 1911 advert for William Buckler, whose factory was on Walnut Street. *(Chamber of Commerce. Courtesy of V. Smalley)*

WILLIAM BUCKLER & Co.

LTD.,

Crown
Mills,
LEICESTER.

TELEGRAMS :
"BUTTERFLY, LEICESTER."

NATIONAL TELEPHONE :
1017 LEICESTER.

CODE : A B C 5TH EDITION.

What my mother did... she used to walk right down Highcross Street and fetch a pram full of this work, you know, bundles of jerseys, and she used to sit up hours and hours right up to perhaps eleven o'clock at night. She's always done it, she'd always worked either cleaning or something at home if she couldn't get a cleaning job. It must have been hard work.

Then I'd had enough of those, so (in 1936) I walked to the Liberty. I says, 'Any jobs?'... they says, 'Yeah, when can you start?' I said, 'Monday.' Then I went on my own time when I was 16. £5 a week I earned, that were a lot of money. The clicking room... they could see the canal and the Bede House bridge. Seen the old man swimming across the Bede House 365 days a year, every morning. When I went in the army you had to go down to Mr Barlow 'cos he was the man. I got five shillings (25p)... a bar of chocolate, writing paper and envelopes, and he shook your hand and you'd think you're everyone 'cos the gaffer'd shook your hand. Everybody that worked in the Liberty and had gone in the forces got a parcel every month.

Good shoes were made there. Portland shoes, that's opposite the old Hawthorn building, mind you they've closed down now, that and the Liberty were the best known for good shoes.

After the war

After the war came better job prospects. Between 1948 and 1974 Leicester's economy grew and work was easier to find.

The big benefit to the working man was the war. Bad thing to say but when they come back from the war - now you know in the First World War they come back... and the bulk of those chaps couldn't get a job - but when this war finished, whether they had spread their wings and got overseas orders I don't know, there was work.

It was after the war... there was a feller from the navy, he'd got called up and he went back to Bentleys and we met... he says, 'Why don't you come down to Bentleys?' So I did, I were there for 30 years. I enjoyed it while I was working there. Actually, compared with other engineering such as Stibbes or Mellor Bromleys and that, I don't think the money was quite so good as there but I enjoyed it. I were only walking five minutes either way and came home for dinner. We used to have a snack and we always had a meal... about five o'clock.

When Bentleys came out it was just one mess of bikes coming up New Bridge Street.

Factories, oh crikey. The first factory I worked in was Poole Lorimer and Tabberer, I was a runabout. You just left school at 14 and went and got a job, not if you can get a job, get a job. You went there, 'Yes, start on Monday'. You'd finish school on Friday, you'd have your week's holiday and you'd start on the following Monday and I think I got twelve and six (62p) a week and that was 8am - 6pm. We had an hour dinner.

They were factories so that people went to work and got home at lunchtime and you went home from school at lunchtime and your mum was there. Even my mother did this when she was in munitions - would be home at lunchtime - and my dad came home and we all had lunch

together and then they'd go back. It was our job to wash up and then go back to school.

I had an aunty worked there (Harrison Hayes) for, I think, 60 years. You mainly all walked to work. A lot of them worked in these factories, you know, like Swanns or Bentleys... but there's some worked in town. There's not so much fun in it now, we all know that, you know. Years ago if you didn't suit in a job you'd either get the sack or leave and you walk round the next and got another job, see. We went to Narborough Road school and I can say most of 'em in my class at school have all ended up with good jobs, you know, and we were only secondary modern.

From about 1959 - 1964 I was down there almost everyday as part of the (Gateway) school and Morleys. Morleys itself was an incredible place. Real old fashioned type of hosiery factory. When I was there most of the manufacturing side had gone but it was an enormous place being used as a warehouse, but it couldn't have changed for about 40 years. Everything, the equipment, the desks, the people, was as if nothing had changed from the '30's. Morleys was I think one of the biggest employers in the area when the manufacturing was there.

I worked at Freeman Hardy and Willis before I got married. I worked at Benjamin Russells as well when I left school. I loved it... £2 6d (£2.02), that were my first wage. You didn't pay board, you gave your parents your wages and they gave you so much to last the week. Then when I moved from Benjamin Russells... to Freeman Hardy and Willis, they were paying £3 15s (£3.75), I thought that, ooh, that were a great huge wage for me.

Not worried about jobs no, I think that came... a lot of the area when they pulled all this down and then people had got to go further afield for their jobs. I think that's when it started going down, 'cos they took a lot of industry away from the area. Specially Freeman Hardy and Willis, they had quite a lot of workers. A lot of local people worked there. Course when that went all these people had to go out elsewhere looking for a job. Too many people after so many other jobs.

There used to be a shoe factory next to the Regal cinema and I can remember standing, I used to stand for hours looking in this factory and it was all sort of like wooden floors and staircases and they used to stand there cutting out or stamping out the leather soles for shoes and I used to think I'd go mad if I had to stand there all day and do that.

I did work at home as well... I had a big industrial machine stuck in the living room. We made umbrella covers and it came all the way from Bradford - because that's how much work they'd got in them days. You'd walk out of one job one day, walk into a job the next day.

Smut!

While there was a lot of industry in the area there was also a lot of dirt coming out of the factory chimneys. If there was a factory at either end of a street, it didn't matter which way the wind blew, the soot got everywhere. There used to be similar problems with the Infirmary chimney.

I never heard anyone comment on the factories and the smoke they put out, which were still active at the end of a lot of roads in the Nuts, because that meant someone was earning money and it was an income and you don't knock something that is actually giving an income to the area. And yet that would be seen as an environmental hazard to their health. There were a lot of very dirty factories down there.

There was quite a hoo-ha and a petition actually, the whole of New Bridge Street area was plagued by the Royal Infirmary's chimney. In those days it was a solid fuel boiler... and they used to burn everything, you name it they burnt it, and you used to get all this grit come down on everyone's washing and there... were a couple of petitions organised about it. You could actually sweep it up it was that bad. It used to happen all the time... there were no clean air regulations. In fact at lunchtimes and in the mornings they always used to sound hooters and things... especially Bentleys and this hooter thing could be heard all over the area. Quite a few of the factories had got them.

The smuts and that from the Royal Infirmary chimney, they were unbelievable, you put the... baby out in the pram and I honestly said they used to come back and they'd be covered. We had terry nappy towels and you'd hang them out in your yard, look beautiful and white, you'd go out, the sun had been shining - you'd have to wash them all again - they were covered in soot and muck. They did pull that down and build a new one.

A VE day party in Middle Street. (Mrs Howes)

WALNUT STREET AT WAR

The sky was red

Many people still remember the Second World War. This first quote is from one of the few who recall World War I

I remember the First World War vividly. I was four years old when that started. My oldest brother who was twelve, he came in and he said, 'Come on let's go and show you the gee gees.' Went to Mill Lane Bridge and we sat on the parapet wall there and they were coming down from the Newarke. I've got a photograph of it somewhere...

They stopped on the Boulevard for a while then they got themselves together and they came round Mill Lane Bridge, along the Eastern Boulevard, around Walnut Street into the sidings, railway sidings, where Berry's yard is now, then by train to France.

I remember Hohenzollern Redoubt (a WW1 battle in 1915) which was a shocking thing for the local regiment. I always remember women running into each others arms when the casualties were published. The Mercury man used to come round with a black edged border poster, terrible time. The privation of the ration, that sort of thing. We made do mostly with vegetables and what meat they could get and I do remember once that my father had acquired a rabbit and my mother when she cooked it, refused to have any because she said she didn't think it was a rabbit, she thought it was cat. It could have been possibly.

I can remember the landmine dropping on Victoria Park (in 1940). Where we lived in Clarendon Street we were in our air-raid shelter which had been built in our yard... and the whole thing shook and that is a mile and a half away.

My father was a divisional air-raid warden and he gave me responsibility from the age of ten for the family because as soon as there was an air-raid he had to go out and he instilled in me I was the man of the house, at ten, and I had to get the whole of the family with the suitcase with food and water into the air-raid shelter, and if there was a bombing coming near I had to strut the walls and all sorts of things - get timbers and sort of shore it in case anything came down. A lot of them had the Anderson which was half sunken curved tin and they just filled with water so most people gave them up.

There was the lady who lived one side. When the war was on every time the sirens went mother said that she could use our air-raid shelter. And she used to, without any sort of by your leave, as soon as she knew she could use it she used to come down through the gate... wrapped in an eiderdown and she had all her worldly goods under that eiderdown and she would sort of go and make herself comfortable in there. We were quite friendly but it wasn't a question of forever in one another's houses.

But I mean we didn't really have a lot of bombing here. I can remember watching Coventry burn from the front door step. We stood on our front doorstep looking over to the west and the sky was red and that was Coventry going. I can remember D-Day, there was a clear night, I'd gone to bed

The press reported this as 'Remains of a dressing room at a Midland city football ground which was bombed last night'. Local people would have known it was the City ground. (*Leicester Mercury*)

and we heard these planes and I got out, looked out of my bedroom window and everybody was out, you could see everybody... and everywhere you looked you could see a bomber towing a glider - everywhere you looked. The sky was absolutely full, it was a fantastic sight, I shall never forget it - because the next day day I'd got diarrhoea so I was off school and I can remember sitting there... listening to John Snagg saying, 'The Supreme Allied Commander will be making an announcement.' I can remember that so clearly.

At the beginning of the war they'd set up British Canteens... that was where they did catering en masse. The British Canteen for us was at the bottom... in New Bridge Street at St Andrew's church rooms which was between Aylestone Street and the next little street... but my father would never go and eat in there, he wouldn't eat in those sorts of places - he would never go in a Working Men's Club either. We used to have to fetch his food from there in basins.

During the war... I've walked in snow inches deep down to the gas yard to see if they'd got coke in and you were only allowed a hundred weight at a time no matter how many kids you'd got. That one at the bottom of Aylestone Street, he was coal, but he did go to coke but he wouldn't get it in very often but when he did the word used to spread like wildfire and he'd be sold out in half an hour.

You had compulsorily to do fire watching at the big factories, you couldn't do anything about it, everybody had to do it at least one night a week. I had to do it at a little factory in the Infirmary Square. You'd got a bed in there of sorts... providing nothing happened you could get your head down.

Filbert Street I were in during the war. They dropped incendiaries on the Tigers ground... and there were two big craters, there were two bombs dropped down the bottom of Filbert Street. Holes in the road, 'cos we went down to have a look at them.

We... used to go down the pub cellar - Queen Vic cellar. Me and two other girls went in first-aid so of course we used to walk the streets. Father Gilman from the church used to walk with us.

Standing in with the Yanks

The US 82nd Airborne Division was stationed in Leicestershire before the D-Day landings in June 1944.

On the county cricket ground... that's where we used to play, I mean... in the war nobody bothered with that so much... and then the Americans had it. They had some troops there for a while.

It was great fun to go down if there was a fight. There were usually fights at The Lifeboat Inn which was in New Bridge Street just between Chestnut Street and Walnut Street. It was a more modern pub than the rest and that was the one the Americans tended to use and there were always punch-ups there, and you'd get down there as soon as you could to see the jeeps arrive with the police with their white puttees and their white belts swinging their truncheons against the side of the jeeps and then they'd swing them into the fellers. And of course the girls liked them as well 'cos they... had the money. The expression in Leicester was, 'She's standing in with him'. It's a lovely expression isn't it, 'She's standing in with the Yanks'. Quite a lot of them were married women as well, whose fellers were away in the forces, I mean, I'm not condemning them.

At the beginning of the war... the 1st Leicesters were billeted in our area around Walnut Street through to Clarendon Street... in all the houses round there. They were the first to go out to France. I think most of them were wiped out.

Three of the girls in this street (Grasmere Street) married Americans and are now living in America.

I do remember that someone I knew had a child by one of the Americans and she was only in her teens.

The Queen Victoria in Crown Street. Pub cellars sometimes doubled as air-raid shelters. (*M & J Zientek*)

I remember some of the girls who'd been going out with Americans coming into school in the morning, throwing themselves all over the desks, crying all over the place because the Americans had gone over and they thought they weren't going to see their boyfriends again. It brought it back to me with the D-Day celebrations on the television recently. It was hushed up a little bit and, you know, talked about in whispers, but she kept the baby and her mother helped her look after it.

War work

These women did jobs that would previously have been for men only.

Bentleys turned to munitions 'cos I worked there for quite a while. All I did was - you never saw the finished product - I put this thing under the machine and there'd be like a curly steel come off it, it was red hot and there was water running all the while and it was just like a torpedo shaped thing but it was very tiny - you didn't know what it was for. You had to be 18 before you could go into munitions.

When it came to the war you see I ended up in engineering, you'd got no choice. Armstrong Siddeleys, that's where Sturgess is now. It weren't bad really, I mean, it were a bit rough, you know, it weren't bad considering it was wartime. They were all lathes and drilling machines and all that. I were on the inspection, used to have to measure every part that came off the machines, you know, there used to be about six of us all in this inspection pen... any that were just this tiny bit under, they had to go out as scrap, any that were a bit over, they had to go back to the machines and be turned again. And of course when they were working these machines it were all suds coming out of them all the while you see, I don't know whether it were to keep them cool or what... we wore these shoes with steel toe caps... looked ever so dainty in them but you see if you wore ordinary shoes that soap suds used to rot them.

During the war you see you'd got a choice, you either went in engineering or in the forces. You were sort of forced into it... you'd got to do it. They were a decent lot to work with, it was quite a decent factory. Used to do long hours as well, used to do a month nights and a month days, used to do 60 hours a week. I had a breakdown. When I went to the doctor's he told me it was with nerves, you know. He asked me how long I'd been working you see, how many hours, and I said, '60 hours a week.' And he just looked at me as much to say well I can't believe that. And you used to take no end of fags with you to keep yourself awake overnight. You'd come out of there in the morning you didn't know where you was, with smoking and that, and that's what done it. I felt so bad one morning that I just had to go to doctor's and that's how I finished up. I think there was a lot of people it served like that me duck, I mean, you just couldn't keep it up.

Street parties

Most of the streets in the area held street parties to celebrate the end of the war.

The kids all used to get dressed up in different things. One street party, me and my pal, her mother made us Dutch girls outfits all in crepe paper. When it was... I think it was the final victory day... in Outram Street they had a street party, they had a piano out on the street. Oh we had a hell of a time. I dressed up in my wedding frock, you know, veil - the lot. She dressed up as a sailor and they took photos of us and we had little bridesmaids and all - they palmed these kids onto us to make up the group. And they marched us all round the streets, all of them in fancy dress and we were on the front. And they had a band. Went all round the Boulevard, everywhere. At night time we went to have a drink - 'cos we won the prize for that street, we only got five bob (25p)... but we gave it back to the kids 'cos it was for kids' party - we went in this pub. Ooh and the beer! They kept saying, 'Here's the ones, here's the ones.' Ooh the table were full of beer, everybody were treating us. Well we walked out and left half of it, you couldn't have drunk it.

You took tables out in the street, you know, right along the street. They did in Victoria Street, right from one end to the other.

VE day, VJ day, Coronation. We used to trim the streets up, hang flags up, out the window. The bloke next door, Mr Stevens, we used to have a piano on a lorry and he used to sit up there honky tonking away, singing, dancing. Each street did their own thing.

VE day we had a real party then. Nobody had anything then but you'd be amazed what came out on those party tables and what they were saving up - salmon and peaches and pears. They were all on the street outside my house... I opened my front window and put my gramophone outside and they were dancing and singing.

The junction of Walnut Street and New Bridge Street around 1957. Most of this has been demolished, and the turning on the right is now Havelock Street. *(Leicester Mercury)*

SHOPS

You didn't have to go into town for anything

Most people remember the area as being packed with shops. These recollections span the half century from just after the First World War to the demolition of the 1960s. The area did not change much and some of the shops remained the same for years.

At the corner of Bonners Lane, Fairfax Street and Mill Lane was a tripe shop kept by two sisters, which smelt as you went by. On the other corner was a pawn shop. It was something that one didn't talk about - that you could see the ladies going over - probably Monday morning, big bundle, but they were all what I call honest working class people.

Sherwins, and it was... where the extension to the school is now, that's where the tripe shop was. Every Friday night they'd all stand out there with the jugs and oh, the smell was superb as you went by. I don't know why it was only Friday nights but I don't ever remember it being open any other night - not for hot tripe - they may have opened in the week for the cold.
There was a fruit shop, the man that owned that was a queer old man with a monkey on his shoulder. And so did the lady on the corner... where the car park is now for the Poly, there was a sweet shop and she used to have a monkey there.

Top end of Deacon Street there was a man called Ben Ward who was the bookie. That was before we had bookies' shops. They'd go to his... he was in a shed... at the back of his house, you went down the entry, you might just say walk down by the side way and in there taking bets in his little cubby hole. I lived there for 14 years before I knew that Ben Ward existed as a bookie. Hush hush, you didn't talk about it because if you talked about, the police'd go round and pick him up.

The greengrocery shop which was further up the street (Aylestone Street), a chap called Stan Udlum who was an All England ballroom dancing champion - I should think everybody's heard of old Stan.
There used to be a house... a Mr Cooley or Cowley and he used to charge everybody's accumulators for the old radio sets. I think for a bit of pocket money I used to take the old ladies' accumulators to get them charged. There was a shop on the corner of Aylestone Street and New Bridge Street which... was a grocery shop. Chap called Harry Smith, and his wife was named Nell Smith, used to run it.

You didn't have to go into town for anything. Everybody had everything on tick, they did, it was amazing, nobody ever paid cash, they'd have it on tick 'til the end of the week. Then you'd pay your bill up on Friday night and start again.
When I got married I went into Harry Smith's and he said, 'Would you like me to open your book?' I said, 'No.' 'Cos my husband wouldn't have any of that - he was a bit that way - and

Harry Smith was quite put out about it because, let's face it, you didn't know what you'd had, you could put a couple of bob on and he'd made a profit, nobody knew and he was annoyed about the fact that I wouldn't do it and we had quite an upset about it for a long time. How do you think they made their profit?

There was more time to chat. They didn't seem as if they were in competition. I've been in Worthington's some afternoons and it's been very quiet and Joyce the manageress would say to me, 'What are you doing... I'm just going to have a cup of tea. If I make one will you stand and have a natter with me?' It was a big shop Worthington's was, it was like any supermarket is now but of course they hadn't the frozen stuff, had they.

There used to be a milkman, horse and cart, and it was a white horse. And he would not go by Smith's unless he had an apple or a carrot. Refused to move until Harry came out and brought him an apple or carrot. He used to go off on his own, the milk horse would go from one customer to the next, know exactly where he was going, but he would never go by... and if he didn't come out he would go on the front and help himself, because everything was displayed.

Nobody thought about hygiene and that, did they... he used to put his hooves on the pavement, say, 'Get your feet off'... he wouldn't move. Harry'd shout, 'You'll have to wait a minute while I serve this customer, he's waiting for his apple.' Harry Smith's cat used to sleep in the shop, huge great thing, used to sleep on the counter.

On the corner of Walnut Street and Grasmere Street was the Co-op which Mother used a lot. On the opposite corner was the newsagent's and sweetshop and we had our papers from there. On the corner of Joseph Street and Grasmere Street, that was a corner shop and we used that on a regular basis as well. There was a fish and chip shop... also there was the outdoor beer licence... you took your own jug.

I used to go either with my grandmother or we would go and get it for my grandmother and... then we'd bring it home and she'd put the poker in the fire, get the poker red hot and put it into the beer. I always remember it sizzling. On Walnut Street there was the tripe shop, have you heard about that?

That fish and chip shop at the top of my mother's street, it had got an eating room at the back - Foster's the name were - it was a lovely fish shop. They'd got a big window at the front... and we used to stand there at night when we'd got some fish and chips. You used to buy trotters... you always used to have them with your fish and chips and they were really nice. You could get pigs' feet and all the lot in them days... you used to put them in gravy, you know, when you had stew.

My mum used to knock a big stew up, you know, and put one of these cow heels in it. And when it had got cold after you'd had your meal you could stand your knife in it it were that thick. My dad used to love them, used to always get one from Fisher's up Walnut Street 'cos they were the cow heel and tripe people. Take your jug on a Friday night, get it hot with tripe in it.

Fishers - George Fisher's and Sons Tripe Purveyors they were called and he used to do all sorts of things. He moved from Walnut Street onto the cattle market where they had a processing plant. They used to have all legs off cattle and lay them in huge tanks and cook them. Mrs Fisher used to sell the tripe on a Friday, always a Friday morning... in the gateway.

They had a live eel you know, kept an eel in a horse trough in the building. Course P. used to go and feed it with raw meat... it used to come up like this and take the raw meat and get back in again didn't it. Course you know they all have to go back to the Sargasso Sea to die and of course it was a standing joke, they wouldn't believe me, I said, 'It'll get out one night, it'll go,' and it did and they found it and it were dead.

Very colourful... and friendly. The people were friendly and there were all those lovely little shops, you know, them old fashioned shops there. You could smell the cheese... and there was something about it.

In our little grocers shop where we went - Danvers it were called - they were helpful in the way that if you wanted anything they'd go out of their way to get it for you. We wanted some lime marmalade... and she got a case of it and never sold it you know.

Talking about the price of meat, price of sausage and so on, you know, little old ladies - 'Got some sausages down at Wills, Mrs Grey... penny cheaper than anywhere else' - and the childrens' ailments, mostly all about that that they used to gossip about. In the shops, that's where you got to know your neighbours really. No supermarkets so everyone went to those little shops.

Little things like George the milkman with the horse, one-eyed George, the horse knew the round as well as he did and he always left a sweet on the top of the milk for our little 'un.

You hadn't got self-service, you'd got the individual one to one. Everybody got to know everybody. You'd probably miss somebody for a couple of days - 'Oh have you seen so and so?' If you didn't see them... everybody'd start asking questions... wondering if he's alright or she's alright, and that's how it was, it was just a terrific community, I loved it, I just wish it could have stayed as it was.

On the corner of Kentish Street here used to be Mr Fisher's, he was a milkman. He used to deliver the milk with a pushed barrow and the churn was in the... it used to swing. It did go off, yes, I mean we used to put it in cold water. Very often it did go off. There were another milkman in Joseph Street, the one we had, Mr Hubbard. He was a bit more advanced, he'd got a float and he used to come round the streets with a float perhaps twice a day. You had to go out with your jugs and it was in a churn and he used to have these long handle... either a pint or half pint...

You used to have the milkman deliver you. Instead of paying him you went down round the Co-op and got these silver, like, discs, they called them milk checks and you paid him with them so he didn't have to handle any money. You used to have a Co-op number. I can remember my mother's number now. Course the milkman used to come with the horse and cart then.

The pawnbrokers

To some people there was a stigma attached to pawn shops and they refused to use them. Other people cheerfully went each week.

Opposite the grocery shop was a... I think it was Casey's I believe, and that was a pawn shop. Of course you've probably heard the old story about people even pawned their furniture in the front room to go on holiday. I also saw a lot of workman's tools in there which was sad really, but probably pawned them because of drink or maybe because of necessity. It's silly isn't it really? People used to come and sing in the streets... for coppers, mind you some of them were just trying it on you see.

The pawnshop on the corner of Mill Lane and Grange Lane, as seen from Fairfax Street.
(Leicestershire Museums, Arts and Records Service)

The first job I got, which was a great experience, was assistant in the pawnbrokers at the bottom of Joseph Street, Harry Leif. He was a friend of my father's and he said he wanted more or less an assistant. I started at seven o'clock in the morning and Saturday night were nine o'clock when we finished. And the people used to come from as far as..well, Saffron Lane. And Monday morning we opened at seven and there were a queue outside. There used to be young lads with their suit. They used to come... Friday, go out Saturday and Sunday and it used to be back Monday.

Harry Leif, he told me, and it's the best thing in life and that's why I've never had any credit or anything in my life, he says, 'If these silly people would only live on bread and water for a fortnight or three weeks the pawnbrokers would be bankrupt.'

At that particular time if they pawned anything for a pound we used to give them nineteen and six (97p) - sixpence for the card. And then when they came back the week after, I think it was a monthly basis, within a month, they paid you £1 6d back so you made a shilling (5p) on a week or a month... if you didn't redeem it within twelve months and seven days by law you were allowed to sell it. Well they never gave the person the value of the stuff or anything, I mean, especially if it was watches or jewellery and that, I mean once it had gone twelve months and seven days the pawnbroker were more or less laughing.

I know certain people, I were never involved in it but Harry, the boss, used to go round and people used to... give him the key of the house so they could go on holiday. I couldn't quite fathom that myself but he never said anything. There were certain people come from Stoneygate. There were one lady especially, I mean, she used to come and her husband's gold chain, his fob chain and that, she used to come on Mondays and then used to come back on Friday so he could wear it to go out at weekends with it. She used to call into the pub opposite, The Rifle Butts.

We had a lot of jewellery, a lot, and the police used to come round about once a month with a big list of stolen goods and then they used to go through all that we'd got. (How often did they find something?) Very often! What happened between Harry and the police then I don't know.

The butcher's shop

This man and his wife owned a butcher's shop in New Bridge Street.

1949 I went to work for another butcher for two years then there were a business become available and I took it where we was. In New Bridge Street, the corner of Joseph Street and New Bridge Street. It was a corner shop with three rooms. And there was four butchers in New Bridge Street... all in close proximity. Three rooms upstairs. We didn't live there, lock up premises. The backroom was the kitchen... we had a big refrigerator in the middle room. We had two doors in the shop, we had a corner door in New Bridge Street and one in Joseph Street.

Very industrial, small factories - Mill Lane was all small factories in them days. Just after the war everything were busy. There were four butcher's shops and we all employed a man... the business was there, very busy street. Trade were good. We used to open about seven o'clock in the morning 'til six o'clock in the evening. I mean, Fridays were always a late night.

There were three in Jarrom Street, there were two in Infirmary Square, you see it were like the pubs - there were quite a few - we weren't the only four in the district. Just meat in those days, we didn't sell any cooked stuff, I mean there'd be a pork butchers used to sell the cooked meat and that.

I used to go to market and buy alive in them days. I used to go to Rugby market of a Monday, we'd have it home here at tea-time, have it killed and it would be in the shop Tuesday morning. In the cattle market there were ten wholesalers beside the butchers' association. I used to use the butchers' association to kill ours, but I mean there were little places in them days before it were all pulled down and modernised there, I mean the tripe were all prepared there and you can't realise the amount of work that used to go on.

They were working class families like. It were all top quality meat, the amount of competition we had. We'd have enough to carry a body of beef a week and about six lambs. Everything were pretty general... you more or less bought in the same market so you knew how the prices were and you'd got to keep your prices for a working class district.

When we first started the trade was £78 a week, the takings were, and the first week you took £98 and we thought we'd done marvellous. But you see best topside of beef was four and six (22p) a pound in those days. Now you're talking £3 a pound. It was 28 shillings (£1.40) the rent which was not a lot of money really was it?

New Bridge Street

People were able to remember many of the shops along New Bridge Street. The following is one person's recollections from the 1950s.

If you start right at the top of New Bridge Street, roughly where the Infirmary bridge is now, you came down there. There used to be a sweet shop on the corner of Kentish Street which... only ever opened when it'd got sweets because they were in very short supply and rationing was in. The newspaper shop on the corner of Knighton Street which was opposite the Raglan pub and that was run by a Mr and Mrs Mansfield. Once a year they had a lucky dip sale when they got rid of all their old stock.

On the opposite corner of the Raglan was a shop that was empty for many years and a couple called Matthews took it over as a wool shop. Go down a little bit further and there was a greengrocery shop... Taylor, that was later taken over by our next door neighbours Bill and Lou Grimes.

On the corner of Clarendon Street you'd got Warren's the gents hairdressers... on the left hand side there was a strange little... mucky little shop and a very nice lady called Dorothy used to run it but never seemed to have much stock of any sort. Gambol's the butchers... next to that was Andrews' shoe shop and everyone used to be in Andrews' club as they called it... 'cos no one could afford to pay for shoes outright so they used to pay for them weekly.

Next door... was the fishmongers called Saunders - it always used to fascinate me as a kid. I used to stand and watch him plucking all these birds and things, they used to sell rabbits and everything. A little bit further along there was a home made bakery and cake shop of some type... next to that was Payne's sweet shop. They always used to have a good selection of sweets in there... run by mainly a lady called Mrs Payne... she was a cripple who used to have a crutch. It was taken over by a chubby lady called Mrs Twigger.

After that there was the pawnbroker on the corner of Joseph Street... the name of it was Leif, I'm not sure. On the opposite side... was the Rifle Butts pub and then on the corner of Napier Street was the hardware shop... the shop always used to have this smell of paraffin. When you bought paraffin they had a tank and they used to pump it up.

Next door to that... Nola's cake and bread shop... Dews the chip shop... another greengrocer's shop... a furniture shop of some description, Hopkins the chemist - it was the only chemist - on the corner of Joseph Street was another butcher called Eric's... a greengrocer... another greengrocer shop which I couldn't understand - two sort of greengrocer's shops next to each other... Worthington's... a haberdashery shop, I know Mum used to buy things like wool and she used to buy her knickers and things from there as well. It was run by a lady called Nora Waldren. I used to have to stay outside the shop when my mum was buying personal things in those days.

You went along a little bit further and there was the electrician's shop who used to sell radios and he used to do repairs... Spencer's I'm pretty sure it was. You had to be pretty well off to go in that shop... electrical goods were quite expensive.

On the corner of Garton Street was a grocer's shop that my mother used to use, it was called Hackett's. Another butcher on that corner, on the opposite corner was the Lifeboat pub which was probably the poshest pub of the lot on New Bridge Street. You'd got the bookmakers... I think they used to call them turf accountants in those days, it was called... Kiki turf accountants.

New Bridge Street looking south from Aylestone Street. Warren's, the barber's, is on the corner of Clarendon Street. *(Leicestershire Museums, Arts and Records Service)*

There was the Beauty Spot ladies hairdressers... a shop that always used to change hands, it used to sell fancy goods then it became a shoe shop then it used to sell lino... a shop that used to sell cheeses, bacon, that sort of thing, called Danvers... Rosie's greengrocers shop and also there used to be a cafe on the corner of Walnut Street and New Bridge Street called the Welcome Cafe. I don't know why I can remember it - it's all coming back actually.

The view from the roof of the Colleges of Art and
Technology, looking towards the power station, in 1954.
Compare this with the recent picture on page 84.
(Leicester Mercury)

DEMOLITION

Slum clearance?

The Leicester Royal Infirmary had been buying houses locally, with an eye to expanding, since the turn of the century. The north half of Knighton Street came down in the 1930s, and by the time the slum clearance started the Infirmary owned a lot of property around New Bridge Street. Part of Bonners Lane was demolished in the 1950s and the redevelopment continued until the nurses' homes and Infirmary car park were built on Walnut Street in the late 1970s. The people doing the development were keen to rid Leicester of its slums, and not everyone was sorry to see them go.

Under the 1952 City Development Plan, the area was due to be redeveloped with new housing and industry. Two things happened which changed this. First, it was decided to make the Infirmary into a district general hospital and this, in conjunction with the new links with the medical school at the University, resulted in a need for expansion. Secondly, at around the same time, the Government announced new initiatives in further education. Leicester was to have a Polytechnic, and it was decided to build it around the Technical College.

The clearance programmes led to many problems. For instance, several local businesses had made their future plans after consulting the 1952 Development Plan. They discovered that their new investments were to be compulsorily purchased and demolished. To give some idea of how difficult it was to plan ahead, when St Andrew's church planned access to its church rooms, it had to take into account that in 1965 Jarrom Street was supposed to become a dual carriageway, with Gateway Street ending as a cul-de-sac by the church.

All the redevelopment was done in the name of 'slum clearance', a term that many local people found objectionable. Some perfectly good houses, particularly in Clarendon Street, were demolished so that the St Andrew's development could go ahead as the planners wanted. In the other streets good houses had to be cleared with the bad, otherwise the Infirmary and Polytechnic could not have expanded. As these quotes show, there were divided opinions as to whether the houses should have come down.

I can give you an opinion on that. I got into the building industry when I left school... I was part of a group of people who felt, you know, people wanted to get away from those areas. I really felt everyone else must feel the same, and I couldn't understand why people didn't feel that. You know, let's put them into nice housing estates - I've been involved in building housing estates for 40 odd years and quite proud of it - but in actual fact not a lot of people really did, they enjoyed living in those areas. A lot didn't but there were still a lot of people that enjoyed living in those areas. And certainly my parent's house, with a bit of money spent on them, as we've done in the last few years, they could have been made into very nice little houses. And they were little but they are what people want.

Unfortunately it was wholesale pulling down. The reason for the demolition of their house (Clarendon Street) was that it was on the peripheral area of slum clearance - and it was classed a slum clearance - and it was needed for the development of the Royal Infirmary but the rest was

'Pompous'

I was very heavily involved with it, with architects and, you know, we just thought it was needed. Pompous, in my opinion now, very pompous. I was one of them, yeah. You know, we thought we knew very well what people want, and a lot of architects still do to be honest. There was no discussion, there was no getting the community to say what they wanted, they were just told...

classed as slum clearance. I felt it was quite insulting to call it slum clearance because it was not slum clearance, they were not slum houses they were working class houses, well cared for, in need of a bit of money spending on them, that's all.

Slums - they'd got three things that you could have slum clearance on... that was, no light on the staircase, no indoor toilet, and rising damp... if you'd got that you were classed as slum. Unfit for human habitation.

They were clean... when you say slum how do you define a slum? Filth... these weren't filthy... there might have been old clothes on them... but they were clean. When I say slum, like, down Wharf Street... or the Northfields where I lived... I mean you've got far worse places. It's people that make slums.

You'd only got to look and you'd got to realise that something had got to be done. Havelock Street weren't quite so bad but Asylum Street was pretty grotty and Outram Street certainly was. You realised they'd got to do something. Living in, well, perhaps squalor's a bit strong but next door to it sort of thing. They kept them awfully clean but the bricks were getting to the crumbly stage, you know, obviously they weren't going to last much longer.

Outram Street was awful, yes, they were very poor. I remember it being very dark that street, as being almost medieval, you know. There were very poor construction as well as the actual design. In terms of sort of public health and decency what you don't want is one bedroom leading straight off another bedroom, so you've got some privacy. They got no bathrooms, usually outside toilets and shared at that, but they also had constructional details - a lot of them were single skin four and a half inch brickwork walls, so they were damp as hell... they weren't built on proper foundations - Leicester has a lot of problems with underground waterways and things and there were a lot of settlement on them.

So structurally they were awful and design-wise they were awful, so really there was no future for them. I don't know, in retrospect, how we used to live in quite such a small space. They were just so small.

My mother-in-law's house was beautiful, on Outram Street. She had to move. She wasn't very happy because she'd lived all her married life there. I think she went up Stocking Farm but she said she wished she never moved there.

It was a blow to everybody... I mean, a lot of them were elderly... and they didn't want to see it go 'cos it meant a whole community was being split apart. And there were so many friends and neighbours, relatives, all in one big area and they didn't want to be all separated. I think it was the biggest mistake they ever made looking back at it... in the name of progress. I'd like to know where the progress is 'cos it certainly didn't do this area any good.

Lovely to have a bathroom

It wasn't the case that everyone had to leave at the same time. Before any of the redevelopment started, some families were keen to leave the area and move into the council houses that were being built on the new housing estates such as Eyres Monsell and New Parks. Some people had known for a long time that they would have to eventually leave. For others it came as a shock; they didn't think they were going to be involved. After the compulsory purchase the Council offered people a choice of places to live.

I got married, we lived down New Bridge Street and as I say I'd got three children and we were offered this house (Eyres Monsell)... we were living with my aunty. Funnily enough we'd see these being built and we said oh I'd love one of them... and we got one more or less where we wanted one, we were lucky. Space - bigger house obviously, bathroom, hot water - oh yeah, a lot going for it. I remember when we first brought the children up here they just ran amok, I mean, an empty house, and they cried because they couldn't see us...

Oh delirious, absolutely delirious, because take it in mind we were living with my aunt in New Bridge Street in one... well we'd got the downstairs which was one room and a kitchen and we were all, that was five of us, my husband and I and my three children were all sleeping in one bedroom. You can imagine. You've got more room... inside toilet which we never had 'til we moved up here, we never knew what it was like to have an inside toilet.

Thrilled, oh it was lovely to have a bathroom, oh yes. I think we'd all had enough and it was marvellous to have a bathroom in a modern house, and a garden. I must admit that it all seemed to happen at once, because I left school and started to work and we left Grasmere Street... and I did go through a period when I was quite lonely. I do remember that... but I soon got over that.

I'd grown up and started to see what the better things in life were and I couldn't wait to get out. A lot of people by the, when was it, middle '50s whatever, late '60s, had moved out anyway. My mother never did like the house for some unknown reason, never did. She always felt it was dark and dim and dreary. I think mainly because the Infirmary nurses' home was sort of slap bang at the bottom of the garden and it was... the back room tended always to be very dark. She couldn't wait to go. My dad was always quite content and happy with his lot. He used to go to work... he'd come home, he'd have his meal at night, he'd put his feet up for an hour, read the paper, then have a wash and shave and go up to the pub for an hour, and that was Dad's life really, which it was in a lot of cases. There were people who were still very happy there - they'd been there all their lives. But these were mainly people, perhaps what, late 50s, 60 year olds that were quite happy and content to stay there.

My parents - when they were made to come out of Clarendon Street - my mother wanted to come out yes... she wanted to go somewhere else, you know, have a bit of a garden and have a bit more privacy. Father never did. And when they had to come out he wanted to go into another terraced house. I remember going with them to look at houses and I said, 'Look Dad, for goodness sake, you've got an opportunity now, you've got a bit of money, you can go into something better.' But he really wanted to stay... he felt safe there, I think that's what it boiled down to, it's what he knew.

I don't think we had any inkling really, not like it is today, there wasn't that much information given out really. More interested in getting on with our lives... then suddenly they were going to start, everyone was moving... and they started knocking the houses down.

We all got a letter - compulsory purchase. It was dead out of the blue, we didn't know much about it at all, only just a little bit in the Mercury my husband read out - it was all going to be redeveloped at the Infirmary. Fair enough, we'd sat and watched them pull all the other side of New Bridge Street down but we still didn't think they were going to touch us because we saw them build part of the new Infirmary, the boiler house and that, and then they started putting these flats up and they put these temporary wooden shops up in Walnut Street, I mean we never dreamt that they were going to take us over as well. We thought we were safe this side of New Bridge Street 'cos, I mean, they'd half built those flats before we got the letter. We all thought, oh it'll never happen to us. I felt really ill, I did feel ill... I just couldn't believe it.

From what I understand from my mother the writing was on the wall for demolition from the time they moved in the late '30s, early '40s. It was always on the cards that the Infirmary wanted to build on there and it was owned... on the rent book I believe it said Leicester No 1 Hospital Management Committee, so there were always plans for that area for the Infirmary.

They thought they were safe until suddenly this order comes that they're going to be cleared out. I actually did get together with a group of them to get better compensation for them. We fought the City Council and got much better compensation than they would have got. They didn't want to leave.

I saw the other side of New Bridge Street, we saw all that come down, I mean, Worthington's shop and all that disappeared so that there was hardly anything left for us to shop there. I was very very sad when I had to leave my home because I'd only lost my husband the year before.

The arrow points to a sagging roof in Outram Street in 1959.
(Leicester Mercury)

They came and told me I'd got to move. I wanted a two bedroomed house but I was told because I was on my own I wouldn't be able to keep the gardens going which is ridiculous. I says, 'Well don't talk rubbish... I've got two sons.' 'Ah well, they may not always be able to help you.' I thought, that's ridiculous. But anyway I was offered a flat down on Caversham Road...

I think we got somewhere around £300 - that was a lot of money. You'd got to pay for your own moving. It was a complete laugh you know, when I moved, because the gas and electricity and the water came and cut me off on the Friday afternoon, now I wasn't supposed to be moving until the Sunday. My daughter came down... and I went home with her. My daughter went with her husband and loaded one lorryful and then the football came out so they decided to leave it and pick the rest up on Sunday. Well... Auntie Pat told me afterwards that they'd not been gone very long with the lorry before the men came to board it up. She says, 'Excuse me, what do you think you're doing... if you look through the front window the lady's still got half her furniture in there.' They were so quick to come and board you up.

Auntie Pat had more guts about it than me, she says, 'I'm not going until I get what I want' ... and let's face it they weren't going to knock the house down on top of her and they couldn't forcibly eject her... it would have been such a stink in the paper. Eventually she got what she wanted... a lovely little house up Narborough Road. A lot of us just gave way... went with the flow sort of thing.

I didn't like my flat, I'll be honest, it scared me, I didn't like it one bit. The flat itself was alright... but I still felt that I'd left my husband and all my friends had gone - I felt lost. I'm sorry to say that I got agoraphobia for about five years. It all stemmed from that - we were such a close knit community...

When we were told that we'd finally got to come out of there I had that house done from top to bottom. Every bit of paper scraped off, new plastered kitchen and everything. It was lovely. Everybody that walked in would say, 'I never knew these were like this inside, aren't they lovely.' When it... was statutory... everyone was being moved out piece by piece and we owner-occupiers we were all informed by letter you see that we had to make a move. The council were very good about you being choosy. I know people that were shown council houses in three or four places and said, 'No we don't want to come here'. And they were very patient as long as you didn't... overdo it I suppose.

They kept saying it had got to come down, then it was standing up, then it was coming down, then it was standing up. At one stage a lady that lived in a little shop in Jarrom Street, Maggie Monk... she asked me if I should like to change when she'd got to get out of that little shop... and go on the estate and her have this house. She said, 'I'd love your little house' , and we'd just had it done through, all the lot. So we said yes, we'd go.

You have three choices, no, two choices. We went and seen it. You went down a step, the hedge was up there you see... your window was below the hedge. I said, 'No, I couldn't live here.' Eyres Monsell I think it was... at any rate we didn't want that. They gave us another one... it was filthy, absolutely filthy... an old fellow had lived there on his own. I said, 'I couldn't go through it... I've just done this lot and I couldn't start...'

So she told 'em you see, she said, 'I don't know how you've got the gall to give a girl different houses like that.' 'Cos she'd already told them she were going to swap. So they said well we don't generally do it but we will do it this time, we'll give you another choice. Do you know where it was? Hughenden Drive in what they had during the war, you know them pre-fabs. I said, 'No way.'

She played hell... she called them everything. So that fell through and it's a good thing it did because just after that they had the floods and some of them that went out of Joseph Street went in them and they lost everything, everything was ruined, carpets, the whole lot. You see they just wanted to push you anywhere... to get them out of the houses.

My mother wanted to go to Thurnby Lodge 'cos my sister lived up there and she got a bungalow up there so, I mean, she got what she wanted but a lot of people didn't. I mean, I spoke to them when they first moved up, you sort of, 'Oh, you're up here', and they didn't like it 'cos it was too open, they'd been used to living in such close proximity with everybody... well they moved up here and they didn't know anybody, they were like fish out of water. It was frightening for a lot of the older ones - for the young ones it was great - but for the older ones that'd lived down there all their lives some of them, it was a big upheaval. Whereas you could just sort of nip out your front door and you were there, now they'd got to walk quite a way for some of them to walk to the shops - well, the shops weren't there - they used to have to wait for the bus to come round - well they couldn't get used to that. It took them a long long time to get used to it.

You soon got to know people, especially with children, because they'd all got children, they were all in the same boat sort of thing, new families and all that. I think children enable you to meet people. There were none (shops), there used to be a van come round which was alright I suppose but it was a bit expensive. He sold everything though - Mr Pinky we used to call him... he used to come out two or three times a week. I wasn't homesick, no, because I loved it, this was mine, it was my first home really, plus the fact that, I mean, I went down to see my mum every week anyway... at least once a week.

Mill Lane was cleared so that Leicester Polytechnic (now De Montfort University) could be built. *(Leicestershire Museums Arts and Records Service)*

Being near the town, them shops, just being five minutes away from the town, and the hubbub of life for me. I mean, the bus routes from Glen Parva were absolutely appalling then. Awful, I didn't like it, I wanted to move back, I said, 'Take me back down to Walnut Street, I don't like it up here I want to go back.' But we couldn't you see, there was nowhere to park a car. You could stand there for half an hour, three quarters of an hour before a bus came, I mean, you'd got two kids with you, standing there waiting for a blinking bus.

What people were left, they were all moved out onto the estates. There were some elderly people that had been there for years and years and a lot of them... they didn't do any good. There was one elderly lady who lived on the corner... and they moved her and she went mental and she was quite alright when she lived there. There was one elderly lady... they moved her, and her son told me he had to go up into this new bungalow they were putting her in because it was drenched with water, the water used to drip down the walls. And he used to have to go up and light the fires and everything to dry it out before she could go in it. And down that road there were no lighting, the roads hadn't been done properly and she used to get her grandson to bring her down to see me but then it got too much for her and she didn't last long. She died.

Staying up, going down

By the mid 1960s articles started appearing in the Leicester Mercury arguing that too much attention had been paid to demolition and too little to improvement. It was recognised that most 'slums' had been cleared and many of the remaining properties were structurally sound. The Winifred Street flats were an example of how it could be cheaper to improve buildings than to demolish them and build again. The Council decided to offer improvement grants to modernise some of the remaining houses, but it was still planned to demolish others around Walnut Street. Many landlords expected their houses to come down but, because redevelopment moved so slowly, no one was sure when. Established families moved out and were replaced by whoever needed cheap accommodation. Uncertainty set in. The demolitions left untidy wastelands and the area began to look run down.

Say 35 years ago... there were three houses became empty in Clarendon Street and the Council bought them and did them up. Before they let them they opened them up for people all round here to go and have a look at them, and if you wanted anything doing like was done in these houses you could get a grant of half the cost. All that's been done here, apart from the bathroom, I've paid for myself. We had the bathroom done and we got half towards that. That, believe it or not then... that were £320 and we got £160... but the clause, if you sold within 20 years you had to pay what you'd had off them back. Quite a lot of them had it done.

I used to ring the Council everyday... and I had a phone call. He says, 'You've put an application in for Eyres Monsell flats, a pre-fab on Hinckley Road or Clarendon Street.' I'm going, 'Clarendon Street, Clarendon Street!' He says, 'When can you pick the keys up?' I says, 'Now... what time do you close?'... They offered us New Parks, Beaumont Leys, Mowmacre, I said, 'No, you're putting me out, I don't want to go.' I wanted to get back in this area, 'cos I like this area, I don't want to move, I know everybody round here, everybody knows me.

We'd been here a few years... and then all of a sudden everybody had got to have a bathroom. The house was rented and it was under Jarroms. We've been lucky with builders - I think we've had some of the biggest cowboys in Leicester. They sent us a feller to put this bathroom in. At the time we'd got a pantry in the kitchen, the bathroom were over that you see... I opened the pantry door and whoa! The water, it were just cascading off my shelves in the pantry. I said, 'What on earth are you doing? I wanted a bathroom putting in not a bloody fountain!' It spoiled everything in my pantry... and he started to laugh, he said, 'Oh I bet we've left the taps running in the bath.' We got the bathroom eventually. The landlord had to pay it. They used to put the rent up every so often and I think it went up when we had the bathroom put on.

The Council said that if they changed their mind (about demolition) we'd all be given a grant... and the little one up one downs would have to go because they were not regarded as hygienic... But they didn't. We knew before we went in to get a mortgage from the building society, the building societies knew, they'd got an insight into what the Council were going to do - 'Oh no, sorry, can't lend you money in that area those will eventually be coming down.' Guess what they did to me. I had a bridge loan from the building society for this (her present house) and the Council never paid me for Walnut Street, they said I'd got to wait six months. And I'm paying seven per cent on the bridge loan. Not until they were ready.

It was very quick... an overnight exodus sort of thing, everybody had gone. Within a matter of months it had all gone - it was gone, it was just rubble. Not months was it, weeks. We used to go by on the bus and one day Aylestone Street was standing and then you could go down the next week and it was just a pile of bricks. You think, oh look, and it was horrible... it was horrible to go by and see it. I used to cry every time I went by on the bus. Our C. used to say to me, 'You are stupid Mam.' Of course, being a young fellow he couldn't understand it.

You can imagine what, nine or ten streets and all the rubble, it really was an eye-sore for ages. And for a short time we had these... itinerants all out here on the back. In the end they had to pile the rubble up at the sides so they couldn't get on. It's certainly improved the looks of the place now.

The corner there, Guiseppe's, used to be a coffee bar. In fact that was in the Sunday papers once, I think it must have been the 1964 election. They had a big poster there - 'Britain's getting better with the Conservatives' - and where they'd put the poster all Guiseppe's, well it were Joe's then, all his windows were broken, all his washing hanging out, it looked really derelict, downtrodden, and then somebody from the papers picked this up and made a good angle. It was in one or two of the Sunday papers, this poster of Britain's getting better with the Conservatives with the backcloth of this run down old cafe with the washing hanging outside and all his broken windows.

They were closing the pubs down, that's why I moved from pub to pub. People kept saying, 'Why do you keep changing your pub?' I'd say, 'Because there ain't one there now.' It used to be a laugh. I was in Walnut Street when they pulled these down... 'cos they were the last few houses right in front of my gateway when they pulled them down and thousands of mice ran out and I was sweeping them out my gateway. All these mice shot across Walnut Street. The solicitor said you'll be alright because it's on the plans - not slum clearance but for road widening. So if they'd have road widened I'd have got the full market value.

We used to have a grand old time. I remember I built a shed for my first scooter out of old doors which came from there. No, I built the shed for my bike... I think Outram Street was probably the last one to be demolished, that dates it around 1967, as late as that then. It was progressively demolished rather than all being flattened at once as I recall. There was no trouble in Grasmere Street but it was part of the kids' game wasn't it, as soon as the houses became vacant you'd go round there and break all the windows, that was part of the fun wasn't it, they were going to be destroyed anyway.

I did go up to the planning. Originally Jarrom Street was going to be widened... they were going to take the first two houses so that meant 132 was the last house in this street (Clarendon Street), well a lot of people objected to that. That never came into force. It could have been the middle '60s. 'Cos the lady who lived at 132, she said, 'What're we going to do?' I said, 'Well just object to it... if they start at that then these houses'll come down... we don't want it.' And then they just shelved that. I wanted to know if these houses were coming down because at the time... about 18 years ago, they asked if we wanted to buy. I went to have a look at the plans, I says, 'Are they coming down 'cos we're not buying if they're coming down.' Not for another 30, 35 years. Well that'll be another 20 years now.

You didn't even have cold water - there was a tap in the yard. Oh I thought, I can't stand that, I'm not having this. Funnily enough I've been a Conservative all my life but it was a Conservative council and he refused when I first approached. 'Oh no they'll be coming down, no no, it might collapse, it might do this...' . The next time voting came and the council changed, guess what? 'Of course, if you want to improve' - and I got it in about 18 months. Very funny indeed that was. They weren't on the statute books or something, they were just in the plan you see.
My solicitor said just as a guess... I would give it 15 years, and what a good guesser he was - that was how long the property was up - 'cos I moved out after ten, and the council let it. This was when they were already moving some people out onto the estates very gradual you see. I was desperate to have my own home then even if it was only for ten years. I'd have never gone into there if I'd had more money.

The man who comes up to me garden-wise in Walnut Street, they were going to take all that down - this was the rumour. I was told in the hostelry that we would have a road or something or a wall belonging to the hospital at the bottom of our garden. Because Walnut Street was going to be taken. The man who lives there now told me this himself, he paid £100 for his house - that was all cash, he borrowed it off his mother - because it was going down and they would have to find him a council house and it didn't come down did it? 'Cos they've been there... that would be going back at least 21 or 22 years.

They were buying them up... for pulling them down... the council. The chap gave me a price, I'll never forget it, £1,400 for the house and I said, 'Right, we'll sell it.' And then he was taken ill, this feller from the council, and they tried to back down on it - no he never said that. We got it plus they paid our expenses as well for causing all the trouble. It's never come down, it's still there now.

The remains of Crown Street, Kentish Street, Albert Street, Victoria Street, and, running top left to bottom right, New Bridge Street, could still be seen in 1973. *(Leicester Mercury)*

THE UNCERTAINTY OF IT ALL

A view from outside

A health worker reflects on what life was like in the area before the St Andrew's estate itself was built.

There was a lot of very cohesive families in the area still at that time where you'd knock on a door, say to visit after a birth a young mother with a new baby; no reply, and someone would hang out a window down the street and say she's gone to her mam's round the corner, right thanks very much. And you'd just literally pop round the corner and you'd catch up with the mum there and do the visit while she was with her mum. Lots of families who literally still lived that close to each other.

I worked it on foot... you walked the streets so to speak... people were very welcoming. Some patches of it were run down a great deal more than others in '65. I mean, there were some beautifully maintained homes and houses and the two weren't necessarily synonymous obviously, people had beautifully maintained homes in terrible houses and vice versa. But there were some very run down properties that had got the idea they weren't going to be around much longer, the landlords weren't bothered, they were letting it to anyone and the people who lived in them weren't getting maintenance for the property and of course it was going downhill fast.

The thing about terraced streets, close together, with employment at the end of the road or knowing the corner shop at the end of the road is that people have got an opportunity over a period of time to establish that closeness and neighbourliness that I was aware of visiting door to door on my feet in that area. You could stop on the street and talk to so many people. Very few people owned cars and there was far more communication because of that. People having to walk out and go shopping and walk the children to school communicate far more than we see nowadays with people driving everywhere and having very little in the way of neighbourly contact, comparison about child rearing, children communicating walking along together - all of that which I think is something that was a great strength in the area and was of the nature of people's lives at that time really.

There were families with tremendous multiple problems and... young mothers with their first child who couldn't manage - just as I'm sure there is nowadays - when people appeared to have all that support.

I think the danger is that we stereotype this terraced close community image and that wasn't happening in every household. There were people hiding in some of the houses that were run down who were in a terrible situation, isolated, having a child on their own, hiding from their family, hiding from another country, alongside the families that had these networks. So there was the same mixture, thank goodness, as we have in almost any community. And the so-called 'bad families'... were hidden in that community then in my experience.

There was a lot of people coming in from '66 onwards from abroad, no English to be spoken, coming to the lowest rents they could get because they had no income as yet established and landlords waiting to put them up, poor properties and so on, who were very vulnerable and very isolated. That was the first intake from '66 as far as I can recall... it was a first port of call for quite a few families.

The bad (houses) would be that you'd look up through the ceiling and see the sky and you'd have multi-occupied even in the little terraced houses. You'd have a cooker on the landing so that people in the different rooms could come onto the landing and use the cooker and go back into their rooms - they had padlocks on the doors. The houses that were parallel going down by the Royal. Knighton, Aylestone, Napier, that's right, those little terraced houses along there, a lot of them were multi-occupied and then you'd get a family in one, you know, who'd been there all their life, highly respectable, clean and well organised and the house was in good order, then you'd go back to another multi-occupied range of houses, so it was very mixed.

People with families who were fairly stable or older people who'd lived there all their lives were quite shocked at this amazing turnover but it was the nature of properties that might be knocked down. The dangers were child safety, fires, falls because of the lack of maintenance of stairs, the damp in the rooms... so there was asthma and bronchitis - asthma wasn't so high on the agenda years ago because bronchitis was more prevalent.

It's symptomatic of an area spiralling downhill fast because it knows its future. They'd reflect on, you know, what's happening round here, we can't go out at night anymore, that sort of thing, and how it used to be much safer - the sort of pattern you'd hear with anyone who feels threatened by change obviously.

Taken in 1977 from Walnut Street, this photo shows the wasteland left when Aylestone Street, Napier Street and Chestnut Street were demolished. This is now the Infirmary car park. *(Leicester Mercury)*

Ignore the hospital completely and ignore the health services because although I was part of that there was no infant clinic or doctor on the whole of that complex at that time. There was no GP and even what was called then the infant welfare clinic was held on New Walk... you had to come all that way with the babies to get cheap milk, vitamins, immunisation, have the baby weighed. That's a heck of a trudge. And there was nowhere we could identify to run a clinic down there at the time. It's taken ages to get a GP service down there, which there is now on Walnut Street obviously but that's very recent.

Hazel Street School has always served very well as a focus because it's always been a friendly school and even when they didn't have facilities for mothers to get together it was a natural gathering place... and a lot of things have spun off from that into more formal community links since then.

Little palaces?

The St Andrew's estate was built in the 1970s. Vehicle/pedestrian segregation was in vogue at the time which means that the estate is criss-crossed with walkways above the car parks. There was also intended to be a shopping centre in the area. A 1966 planning brief for the area wanted about 20 shops to replace the dozens that were being demolished. In fact, only six shops were built and then only after long delays. This gentleman and his wife ran a butcher's on New Bridge Street and then moved to one of the new shops on Walnut Street.

Forty odd year I was down there, it's a long while... There were only about my shop were left out of the whole district really, with the original people in the area. When we first had notice that we was going to be purchased they said that the new shops would be built and ready for occupation before ours were pulled down and they weren't. You had first refusal because you were being compulsorily purchased. Several of the other shopkeepers were near to retiring age which we weren't. There was only two of us when it came to the move... they just didn't did they? They just disappeared. We were looking for property, 'Oh no, it's all coming down, right from Mill Lane to the power station, it's all coming out', you know, then the next thing you know it's all got squashed, they're starting to pay money to modernise the places. You see that were the trouble... nobody had got no certain figures... the uncertainty of it all.

Well we knew you couldn't do nothing about it, you know, I mean, the thing is I were young enough to... you just took that chance, I mean, they told us we were going to have a Portacabin for twelve months and we were in it for eight years, so we managed in a Portacabin in Walnut Street for eight years and we kept the business together. Where the boiler house is now to St Andrew's, we were on the front, there were five shops there, or six. The shops were built and they weren't fit to use, ours weren't. To start with they were underwater, the floors were... it was building faults I suppose really. We had two new floors in ours... the concrete all just... disintegrated. Each shop was just a shell, you had to put everything in yourself, including the lightbulbs. I just can't remember how long it was until we complained about the floors. We had no end of trouble about that. The health inspector came because it was breaking up, he said something's got to be done about this, you know, we got hold of the Council then and they did come and sort it out. They just said it were our machinery that were heavy, then after consultation like, they found it were the concrete itself... it wasn't of the quality it ought to have been. Originally they did put tiles on the floors... and they said that wasn't satisfactory... that was another cock-up. We did have several meetings with different people to try and get more parking spaces for the shop but nothing materialised.

We noticed we were losing all the shopping area, that was the biggest shock I think, because there was nowhere where they said they was going to build anymore shops or anything, all the shops had gone. They were worried, they were saying, 'Well where's all the shops going to be?' But nobody seemed to do anything about it, I mean there were never any petitions or anything like that.

The great demolition was for the St Andrew's estate and I was working for the local council then in the housing department. What they aspired to and what they got were poles apart actually because that was going to be a class development when it was first put up. You needed references to get flats there and what have you. It just didn't seem to work that way. And now I have to be honest and say I think most of it is the bane of our existence... which is very unfair on the few decent families that are there.
It was going to be the pride and joy, everybody was absolutely convinced, and I didn't know enough about things to have a look at plans then but I was absolutely horrified when it was finished 'cos it just looked like a prison, the back... all those dreadful walkways, quite soulless. I think general opinion was that it had really split the community because the community started to go down then and it's never really picked up.

I had to walk... through the building and I mean you'd got stones every which way you know and you'd have to careful how you do it, and then suddenly they were all gone and they start putting the foundations in. It seems as though the pumping out was never going to stop, it was on all the time until you'd got used to it in the end. And then they built them flats.
 Friend of mine got a chance of those flats and the Council wanted to know the last time she took breath, they wanted to see... previous years' rent books, bank books the lot. How long they'd lived in the street, how long they'd lived in the city, all things like that and then suddenly they stopped vetting people. For the first two years they were vetted. I always called it San Quentin. I know my sister lived in Aylestone Street and she was offered one but she says, 'No, in four or five years they'll be slums.' Yet there are some people in there who are absolutely brilliant people... and the flats are really nice inside but they get the same name as everybody else.

Things when they're coming down, it's a sort of devastated feeling that you're never going to see that again. And you try to come to terms because we used to sit in the Lifeboat and watch St Andrew's being built. You could hear the men sort of sitting with their pints and saying, 'It'll be like living in dog kennels won't it.'

Manipulating Money

I was involved with an architect in putting forward a scheme for developing the area at the time - we didn't win it - because it was a competition. St Andrew's, yeah. I was an expert with the 'yardstick', that was manipulating money, getting the right sort of density on a house - you could get a lot of money out of the government - and that's where I was involved with it.

At that time the more houses you could put onto a piece of land that looked good and fitted into the theorist's idea of what people wanted, the more money you got from the government. There was criteria you had to work to but it didn't really involve people.

Not to my knowledge, people were never involved. God, it seemed awful when I went down the bottom of Clarendon Street into the area where all the car-parking is... I mean it's open for violence and things isn't it?

When they really went up they were like little palaces they were, beautiful, I mean, there was central heating, bathrooms, I mean we'd never seen a bathroom you know. We were wondering whether it was possible to put our names down for one of those but at that particular time... I think you'd got to get two or three guarantors... you had to have references and all like that, and there were no pets allowed or anything.

I came back here 18 years ago, '76. They'd have been up what, four or five years I think, and it was great then, even then, it was great round here. It was very hard to get one of these properties on here then... they even came round to check my house... it was the ruling that if you had two boys you only needed two bedrooms, one for yourself and they shared. Now that ruling's completely gone, you know, you'd get three. I was a single mum with two boys then, two young boys. They came round, they wanted to see the house, how I kept it, they wanted to know what sort of insurance - I'd got to have insurance... contents insurance, things like that. After I'd moved in, after a little while I had a visit from one of the Council officers to come round and check that everything was alright. You don't get those visits anymore. They were nice here then, the neighbours were nice, the estate was really clean, really nice to be in. There were children on here but there weren't a lot of overcrowding, do you know what I mean, the children were well behaved. When they first came to the area... they really liked it.

Well you could gradually see it going downhill as regards the rubbish what was being left. It was just a slow gradual downhill... people didn't seem to be bothered about anything anymore, never took pride in anything. You see, used to wipe the stairs down ourselves... besides the cleaners. The cleaners that we had then... they were round religiously, you know, and they came round doing the stairs all the time.

In the meantime if anybody needed any help, like the elderly, 'cos the elderly were all around the... I think that's when it started going down, when the elderly were moved off somewhere. You know, as they died and went and then they were let into flats for the young single people, it seemed to... the elderly kept the community together somehow. I think there were a little bit more respect.

You don't get to know them, I couldn't tell you who lives above me, not got the foggiest clue, I wouldn't know. People are moving in and out that quick you don't get to know who's where or who they are. It's only the old regulars, if you like, on the estate that you get to know.

The view from the roof of the Hawthorne Building of De Monfort University, formerly the Colleges of Art and Technology, looking south, in 1994. Compare this with the picture on page 68.
(C. Hyde)

LIVING IN THE AREA NOW

Collections of individuals

The Walnut Street area has changed considerably in the last 25 years. The final demolition of New Bridge Street in 1974 coincided with an economic slump - from June 1974 to January 1976 unemployment in Leicester increased fourfold. Local factories closed down and many families left the area.

By the 1980s most of the new building had been finished and although there have been changes since - perhaps most notably the Queens Building at De Montfort University, the Carling Stand at the football ground, and the Windsor Building at the Infirmary - the area has not changed too much in the last ten years.

The Welford Road recreation ground, now Nelson Mandela Park, has been improved, but that on Filbert Street has disappeared under a car park. Thirlmere Gardens now has a play centre for young children, Southfields College has replaced some of the allotments, and the cattle market is awaiting redevelopment. In the development plans of the 1960s and 1970s it was hoped that Walnut Street would be widened and would eventually cease to be a major through route. When the recent Evesham Road scheme was cancelled these hopes were squashed. Although there have been various grant schemes to improve the housing in the area some people feel that, in the eyes of the Council, Walnut Street has been became a 'forgotten area'. We asked people what it has been like living in the area in the past few years. The following quotations are negative in their outlook, but few people had anything positive to say.

Of course some of the problems of the Walnut Street area are just symptoms of life in the late twentieth century and are experienced in most modern cities, but many are specific to the area. On their doorstep local residents have a university, a hospital, two sports grounds, and, bisecting the area, a busy main road. The problems caused by these institutions are highlighted in this chapter. These first quotes show how previous schemes to improve the area left residents disillusioned.

> *Collections of individuals. I mean, there's a few people who are out on their doorsteps polishing their front door knockers and sweeping the street and they stop to have a chat now and then but there's no big community as such. I think there's quite a varied mix of people really.*

> *Actually the first time I became involved in the community was at Hazel School when I was working in the community centre, and it was while I was there that several of us got together and thought well, if this Housing Action area bid is going to go through we need a negotiating body with the Council, so... I think initially there were four of us started to set things up.*
>
> *Now this would be ten, twelve years ago. Some government grant where they were doing up areas that were in a bit of a state and re-roofing, new walls, virtually gutting some houses and re-building. It was quite good but it was fraught with problems because several of the contractors weren't very good.*

The enveloping scheme happened in 1986 and the grant scheme happened in '89 I think it was... so we went for a long period of plastered walls, for many years, because we knew the next stage was happening, there's no point decorating. We lived in a half-finished house.

And they never did finish the scheme off because at the end of it all I mean, they were going to do the roads and re-do the pavements because we said please could we have our proper paving stones back. That's what's really made me cross because it's gone on for years and years and years and not been finished and there's no money left now, so when City Challenge reared its ugly head I thought whoopee, we'll get our scheme finished, only we haven't.

They wanted all the money invested into new initiatives and of course obviously for local residents it's extremely frustrating to see projects on pavements, lighting, and drainage go by the board, although I think the drainage has improved since we had it out with them - that must have been about four or five years ago.

Bloody cars! Bloody students!

The main problem in the streets used to be kids playing football. Now it is cars. The streets around Hazel Street have a residents' parking scheme but, as can be seen from these quotes, there is a huge traffic problem. Many local people also see students as a problem. While interviewees had different estimates of how many students there are living in the area one thing is clear, more are coming. De Montfort University is expanding and there are plans for student accommodation on Bede Island.

I think my dad was one of the first people to have a car in that street. He had a car in about 1959 possibly, something like that. I'll bet there'd only be two cars in that street (Grasmere Street) 1959, so we'd just play in the street, never any problems at all. Really, it was only about in the late sixties probably and the very early seventies that there started to be a serious parking problem. In the late fifties, early sixties the Poly... it was very small.

That's one of our bugbears, the parking. It gets to be a nightmare. When City are at home, Tigers are at home, there's something on at Granby Halls, the Infirmary car park's full and the students are here, we're just one ruddy great big car park.

If you leave your car out there (Sawday Street) they tow it away. I can't even park my car outside my front door without getting a ticket.

When I first came here (Grasmere Street) I couldn't sleep, it was just constantly, there's people coming and going, coming back from the pub, noise and everything, but now you just get used to it, you sleep through it, it's just like a natural background noise. And the lorries as well, I mean the lorries go by the house and shake the whole house, it's really quite a bad traffic problem really. They've put in speed ramps but they're hopeless, they really are hopeless. I mean, they slow down to a certain degree but they're still going fast between the bumps, it doesn't really work at all. The only time you might see a few spaces might be a late Sunday evening when everyone's gone out.

In the week you've got all the nurses from the Infirmary, I mean, you won't get your car in here (Filbert Street) after half six in the morning because the nurses are there. They've built this Carling Stand and that, got more trouble now than ever have done... since that's gone up. When they start selling tickets for the big matches people come and instead of going on their car park they park the car here.

About every ten minutes you'll be sitting here, you hear a car door bang, pull away, soon as they're gone another one will... bang! That's what you get. And also, since they've had these seats put in, you see they have a job sweeping it up and they've got some big blowers and you sit here and it's like having your hoover on... and I've got double glazing. It gets on my wick. I usually sit in the other room with this door closed and sometimes if it's not a very good match I don't know they're playing.

City... I'm not too happy about because all their family days - I mean, it's a lovely idea - but we just get no break from traffic at all. We knew that when the stand went up and they were opening all these other wonderful things that they would want to use it seven days a week - they have to make it pay - but you see there's no provision for extra parking. We did remind them that there's a school on their doorstep and the kids would love to go and kick a ball on City's ground and what have you, and their marketing director Barry Pierpoint did take it up and I think there has been odd coaching done at the school. So they are aware of the fact that there is a community, that they do cause aggravation, and they are trying, albeit in a very limited way, to lessen the problem, but I mean...

I mean, down this street I'd say it's about 80% students... there's a lot. We just about talk to our next door neighbours... I mean, I say hello to people and that but we don't really have that much contact because... honest, we've got people living each side of us, I can see then once a month maximum sometimes, you just don't see them... so it's not a case of avoiding them, we just don't see them... 'cos everyone's on courses, going out at different times you just really don't get to see

people at all. At the moment my boyfriend lives a bit further down the street and... I think they've housed somebody next door to him but they're like a really rough family. But there again I don't think they're going to be able to put a particular type of people in Grasmere Street because it's just all full of students... There's a man down the road with a neighbourhood watch scheme but I don't know anything

The new Carling Stand on Filbert Street. *(C Hyde)*

One of the problems of a neighbourhood with a shifting population is trying to make residents feel they have a role to play in the community.

I started the neighbourhood watch then I folded it 'cos I get no backing from this area. The residents, they want everything doing. The residents' association get nobody. I mean, they want everything doing but they won't back the committee and you get a bit sick of it.
I mean, you get stopped in the street, 'When are you going to get these drains done?' Now I just say, 'On the phone, ring the council.'

They're really apathetic - you have 600 odd houses in this area and if you get twelve people at a residents' meeting you're lucky. That's despite everything. At one point, if there was a student problem or if there was a parking problem they'd come out in their dozens, now they don't even bother about that.

about it whatsoever. We are students, people come and go so often... I don't think they really have any faith in students adding to the community really.

It's a moving population and it really has broken the community that we had because you get people in for a couple of years on a course at the Poly, or the Uni, and they really don't care about the area, they're just here while they do their thing and then they're gone. Our old people are getting older and dying, there aren't families staying now.

1979, '78... Kershaw (a student hall of residence) was built across there and I knew a lot of the students then, specially one, Anthea, she was from the north east and... she used to come in here and have coffee and study and then that led to one or more coming in. I called them my kids. Every nationality I've had in here. They respected it, they didn't abuse the place and they looked after me.

I fear more student housing. Touch wood we're very lucky in this street, the students we've got are, in the main, very quiet but there have been horrendous problems over the years. Noise, damage. In the main most of us can remember being young and we're reasonably tolerant but it does go over the top at times.

I know there are students who did actively look after elderly neighbours or check up on them, and actually took a more mature view of living in a society. To say all students are the same certainly isn't the case. I think all new students ought to be issued with an induction pack to the area.

Surprisingly enough very few of our complaints (at the Council) are actually caused by students. What tends to happen is, yes maybe they have the odd party, things, but people tolerate it - students - and if a little old lady comes round and bangs on the door they usually turn it down and behave don't they, as all good boys do. But St Andrew's, you know, where we end up is where people are so just bloody minded they won't listen to anybody else's view on anything... there's usually something behind it all, it's not simply a matter of, 'I want my stereo on a bit loud tonight', it's, 'To hell with the rest of the world and I'll do as I like', sort of attitude. And that's not a typical student thing is it, to be perfectly honest.

St Andrew's estate

Rightly or wrongly the St Andrew's estate, like many other estates, has picked up a bad reputation. Drug dealers, prostitutes; they are all supposed to have lived in St Andrew's at some point. People living nearby have been affected as well. This first quote is how a twelve year old who lives on the estate summed it up.

It's good round our estate and sometimes it's bad but it depends on who you are... what sort of people you are. If you're posh people you probably think it's a dump but if you're dump people already you probably think it's posh.

At the time of writing St Andrew's is being redeveloped

Actually it's what we fought for. The first plans that we saw, what they wanted to do to the estate, was for three, four, five bedroomed houses which anyone with any sense would realise is impractical. We did fight for that, to get more or less what we wanted. We got a compromise anyway so I don't think we did too bad really. So, just looking forward to it happening now. It looks good on paper anyway, let's put it that way.

Your first impression when you're actually looking at the place from the outside, you know, as you enter into St Andrew's, was the shock of... all the stone and the concrete, and there was no playing area for the kids. I used to take them onto the park or over Nelson Mandela - that was the recce then - but that wasn't much cop neither... in those days (1980s), I mean, they've done wonders with it now. But the park (Thirlmere) was even worse, there used to be always broken glass.

If you've got kids going to the day nursery or if you've got kids going to school, on your walk to school in the morning you'd meet people. Most of our kids were going to the day nursery, we'd sit and have a coffee in the mornings, that's how we met and then we started like... started keep-fit things - not that we did much - but we started. Things like that, when it's, like, kids' birthdays and stuff like that you'd have a little get-together. The day nursery's really nice, they've got really nice staff and everything.

All my friends now have moved off the estate and we've all gone to different areas. What I find... is, like, the Council, they seem to push everybody into the same area. So you don't ever got a chance to meet married couples, do you understand what I mean, see people who are getting on and, you know, that are working... all they've done is pushed all single parents in the same... in the one area.

I was told once actually... you know the cat-walk - we call it the cat-walk - that is your footpath and if you walk down on the ground and a car was to knock you over, you're in the wrong because there's no pavement down there... because we were complaining once about how fast cars were going. I tell you what, the amount of kids we've seen... swing, jump, you name it. We are surprised really that none of these kids round here aren't brain damaged 'cos kids do stupid things. We used to have a lot of problems as well with the lifts. You'd get stuck in them with your shopping and the kids... it's not funny! Listen, older folks thought that we shouldn't be on the estate anyway, they thought single parents and kids were a nuisance, like we didn't have any rights to be anywhere, we made too much noise. I was quite lucky, I had decent neighbours - I had black neighbours. But you see... people who live round there moan that they're making too much noise. My own kids were only allowed to play... where I could see them. You don't know what could happen.

It's not stories, it goes on... your prostitutes. The problem is with St Andrew's, right, it's a good little place to do all that stuff, do you know what I mean, it's not out in the open like Highfields, you ain't having to stand out in the street or anything like that. St Andrew's... has got nice closed in little bits for those things to carry on without people seeing exactly what is going on. All I ever said, right, providing they don't do it on my doorstep... or give it (drugs) to my kids and stuff like that then that's their business, if they want to go to prison for x number years, right, then that's down to them.

If anybody asked me where I lived, right, I used to say, 'You know the Royal Infirmary don't you, just off there.' Even when I post letters and stuff I never put St Andrew's on letters, never, 'cos to me, like, you're just dooming yourself. You know you go for a job of anything like that and they put St Andrew's - they got no hope, and as for credit, my God! you'd never get credit. Although we used to get the footballers and stuff through the estate they never really caused any trouble. The kids used to play out on the back and they never touched them or anything. But then this little old man, well, he's not that little and he's not that old - he's got enough sense to know what's right from wrong. The kids were playing out on the green and he dropped a brick on my youngest son's head from his window which was on the second floor. According to him they were making too much noise. I says, 'Well why didn't you come and say to me, look can you move your child, why

St Andrew's estate, showing pedestrian walkways above the parking area.
(Roger Hutchinson)

did you have to drop a brick..,' I says, 'where's the logic..?' One Tuesday night I was cooking dinner and the kitchen window came in, he'd actually shot a shotgun pellet through the kitchen window.

So I just told the Council then, listen I want out. Apart from the heat, you know, all the central heating we had, and all the luxury hot water and stuff like that, no I don't miss anything. Nothing... apart from the fact that you can't park down here (near the football ground). I mean, we have seen a few scuffles outside the doors... but that's all excitement isn't it, we sit at the windows and watch.

We were going to have the estate all changed a few years ago (1989) but then something happened, they went bankrupt or something, and that knocked that on the head. And I think that's why there's a lot of apathy about this estate now... it is being done but people still have that, say, 'I'll believe it when I see it', because they've been let down so badly in the past over different things.

You get the security helicopter around the Royal or around St Andrew's quite a lot but, I mean, it's a minority group and they're the ones who dominate, they live almost, I think, outside society. There's tinges of that on the estate.

WHAT DO PEOPLE WANT?

In 1992 Leicester successfully secured City Challenge funding to regenerate the West End of Leicester. Initial progress was slow, and the cancellation of the east-west link along Evesham Road was a major set back, but at the time of writing there are plans for a new road system, new housing, a new park area, supermarkets, and, on the cattle market site, a leisure complex. Local residents are unsure what impact this will have on them.

Unlike the developers in the 1960s, City Challenge have consulted people in the area about what they want for the future. The two things that everyone we talked to agreed on were the need for a supermarket and the need to tackle the problem of traffic, especially if new projects in the area were going to attract more cars. Also, while it is generally agreed that local facilities for pre-school children are good, there is a lack of facilities for teenagers. This first quote is from a man who works for the Council.

One reason we chose this area for City Challenge was that originally there was a proposal to redevelop Bede Island that had fallen through a few years before. So that was the idea when we knew of the City Challenge bid. Bede Island was the focus... the jewel in the crown that was going to be. There is contamination... there've been scrapyards on that site for a long while now. Say when the river bed was moved in about 1900 the railway had those as goods yards so there's sort of coal slack and all sorts of things. There's also odd bits of land fill gas problems... we think that's to do with the old river bed that's still rotting away underground where it's been buried. It's mostly oils from vehicles that's contaminated with all sorts of heavy metals... and metals themselves from the actual breaking and recovery process.

I've had somebody round to talk to me, he was here about an hour, about what we wanted. He'd got questions on a paper and he gave me a pad of cards with answers on - a, b, c, d, e and I had to say e, or a, whichever I thought would be better. What we're worried about really, I mean, we're overdone with traffic; traffic is a problem and the things they're proposing, they're going to bring more traffic in, that's what's worrying us. When people come to me nobody can ever get in on the front, never. They still don't know what they're going to do to be honest, it's still in the talking stage.

We've got nothing now really. We've not got a butcher's since Eric went... you've got your post office, you got your chemist, which they tried to close that down but... there was a big petition going round, save the local chemist. We've only got corner shops and they're very expensive, they can't help it, they have to be expensive. You know, a decent supermarket would solve a lot of problems. I mean, some of our old dears, bless them, don't get into town at all now and I mean, unless you're hale and hearty it's a heck of a trek to go for food. Most people in this area go to town, or cars - they go up to Fosse Park.

You don't buy no more than you have to buy round here unless you're desperate. I used to do it in town, just take a taxi home. You can catch buses but you can't catch buses with, like, bags, I don't feel comfortable. We used to walk up because you used to have a buggy and you'd have one (kid) traipsing on the side of it. If you were doing your proper shopping for the week then it's a taxi job. And it's like if you used to go up with your friends - because they only live round the corner from you - you'd go half on the taxi fare... so it was cheaper than struggling on a bus.

I consider there's a great need for local shops but at the same time it's not economic to shop locally. If you do have a supermarket... that's going to undercut, through loss leaders, the local shops who will then suffer. The local shops still function in a community sense, there is information passed through shopkeepers... discuss, talk about the weather, local situations. You wouldn't get that with a supermarket, they wouldn't play a role in the area.

Yes, I've been and seen all of it but as I say, I'm nearly 80 now, by the time it's all done I don't think I shall be here. You take the cattle market... it's bound to take a long while to do it. I think it should be alright as long as we can get more shops. If you know this area there's not a butcher's shop round here at all. To do our shopping we've got to go into the town. We've not got a decent greengrocer shop round here. I know we've got a really good bus service runs into the town but... you've got two bags to carry, I mean you can't get onto the bus well when you're getting old, and getting off and that.

It's alright them doing all this up, right, but it's going to bring in more traffic isn't it, and what happens to the kids then? I mean, I like the idea of them putting more into the area... it's going to bring in new people, people who you're not going to know... people that are just passing through, they work round here. That means in another way, right, that your kids are in more danger, 'cos whereas now you can look at somebody - well they live around here - you're not going to know Tom, Dick, from Harry.

You want a community centre round here for the kids especially, keep them off the streets. So I wanted to do it for this corner where the flats are, that was a tip for years (corner of Jarrom Street and Clarendon Street) and I went to this meeting... and I says, 'What about this land at the corner of my street, couldn't we have a community centre built on there?' No, the Council pooh poohed it.

Six shops replaced the dozens that were knocked down. The butcher's has been closed for two years and still bears the name of the last owner.
(C. Hyde)

The Carling Stand looms over St Andrew's Play Association in Thirlmere Gardens. *(C. Hyde)*

I think the problem is it's a very mixed age group as far as the kids are concerned. I mean, in this street they're either very very small babies or they're 17, 18 year olds who aren't interested in what's here because everything's in town for them. Apart from St Andrew's Play Association which caters for very small up to I think about 14 or 15 year olds I don't think there's much else. I think they do a fantastic job, I think the area would be very very poor if they weren't there.

Thirlmere Gardens, when I first moved here it was like, they had tarmacked a large area of it... so you can imagine tarmac with bits of broken brick, stones, broken glass, which were swept up but it looked pretty tatty. The city council approached the residents' association, we overlooked the plans. The park can get heavy, there can be some heavy people or kids down there. When the

The development of the Bede Island site depended on the Berry scrapyard being moved. This interview, with one of the Berry family, happened before the business was compulsory purchased.

They came to Leicester in 1905, that was grandfather who was a builder who left Birmingham looking for work with a horse and cart and decided to set up in the scrap business in Leicester and he originally set up in Bridge Road. And then he, with his sons... moved in here in the mid-thirties onto the Bede Island, albeit further down, and we moved onto this corner in 1959/60. Then three years ago City Challenge started, initially very amicably. But of course the whole thing's changed now, the kid gloves are off and it's CPO. They've even talked of offering us an amount of money to extinguish the business, which we don't want to do because I'm third generation and there's even fourth generation Berrys working in the business now. They found that they couldn't get us an inner city site and get us a licence for a scrapyard. What we think is if the City Council themselves can't get planning permission in the city for a scrapyard what chance have we? A little embittered after all the years and the service we've given the city. I've always had an argument that if all the scrapyards in Leicester closed down for a month the city and county would have the biggest environmental problem they've ever seen. We may be what some people call an eyesore but we're very necessary.

Leisure Centre? Multiplex Cinema? Supermarket? The cattle market sits and waits.
(C. Hyde)

centre's open it's fine but I would still escort them (children) there and escort them back. I think the people who run the centre are marvellous and they do a great job. There should be a lot more resources going into that centre to make it better and serve more needs and open for longer, 'cos there is a real need for it in the area. The long term plan for the future is the International Youth House to provide - because there isn't enough for teenagers in the area - certainly not, there's not enough on their wavelength. It gets very very repetitive, I mean, we've exploited almost everything in walking distance around the area, you know, like the Great Central Way, the canal is a popular one, the BMX track, Welford Road cemetery, the nature area on Freemen's Common... the Raw Dykes.

All they have at the moment is, like, Granby Halls but my kids rarely go there unless it's skating or something like that. Why's that? Because you can't afford it. Do you know what I mean, you can't afford to send all your kids and it's not fair to choose one over the others. Southfields (College), they go to Southfields but they're not welcome over there. They moan about them... I don't think they want kids from the area to be involved in that, it's just there for the members that go to their college. From the age of 14 they can no longer go to St Andrew's play building so from the age of 14 they have nothing to do. My oldest now is 14, there is nowhere for him to go, there is no groups or anything like that... now he's out there on the streets. For the next three years now what is he doing? So this is where I'm going to have the police knocking on my door isn't it.

Looking to the future

With one eye on the University and the other on the Infirmary it is not surprising that residents are pessimistic about the future. The most optimistic people quoted below are those who no longer live in the area.

Clean drains, clean streets, we've been after for years. I'm not optimistic about it. I think with the Poly being on one side and the hospital being on the other we're gradually getting closed out. They will have to take me out feet first. They seem to be dithering... messing about so much... they still don't know what they're doing.

Well, I mean, to be honest it seems... they're more interested in the football ground and the Polytechnic really, De Montfort University. I mean, it virtually will be like a little university town soon and then where do all the people who live round here stand?

Quite honestly I'm convinced that... we're all going to be demolished in the fullness of time to become De Montfort University. I have said this to various Council people and been told it's a load of rubbish. I would go quite happily.

It's hard to say now, I mean it's got to the stage now where whatever they do seems to make it worse I think myself. It's like they've gutted a nice little area and just left little pockets haven't they?

The Infirmary's got to expand in years and years to come because there's more people living now. I think the Infirmary must come this way because it's the only way they can expand isn't it? We're really being crowded out aren't we, but the Infirmary must expand I think.

I think Bede Island can be very nice. I think... the area round the river, they can make more of it. It's a nice part of the city. To my mind the whole area, for a terraced house area... is one of the nicer parts of Leicester, it still maintains its character to an extent. It's not as nice as it was when I was growing up in it but I still feel - maybe it's looking at it with rose-tinted specs if you like - but I still think if I had got to live in a terraced house again anywhere in Leicester, and I know Leicester very well now, that I'd still live in Grasmere Street.

I believe that between the canal and the River Soar you have a marvellous area there for building very good housing... good quality housing for people. A nice area of land there once you've cleared that Frank Berry stuff out... you've got a vast area that really ought to be housing and shops in my opinion, not supermarkets, shops. I don't really feel it should be students' hostels. I think you could mix them up otherwise you're going to get another ghetto and I think this ghetto mentality, it goes back to building council estates just after the war, you built ghettos and you shouldn't do.

Some people do not believe they will see any benefit from City Challenge.

City Challenge... I mean, I spent nearly two years of my life going to and from committee meetings and meetings for this that and the other and this area has got absolutely nothing from City Challenge. The football club has, De Montfort University has, but the real grass roots residents have got absolutely nothing.

Candidly I think all they've done with the monies they've got from central government so far is put in traffic calmers and a bit of grass on the canal bank and create jobs, highly paid jobs, for eight or nine people. I've attended one or two meetings and the biggest decision that's ever been made is whether that have one sugar or two in their coffee. I don't attend anymore 'cos they're just a waste of time. No one appears to be able to make a decision.

Conclusion

At the time of writing City Challenge have purchased the whole of Bede Island North and the way is clear for the redevelopment to start. If their plans go through the area is going to change dramatically and, as can be seen from the above comments, there is uncertainty as to whether the local population will benefit from these changes. In the past three years, as during the redevelopment 30 years ago, rumours about what is going to happen have been rife.

I was out on Saturday... and the women next to me, she was saying, 'Were you ever ashamed to live there?' I said, 'No!' 'Were you ever ashamed to take anybody there?' 'No.' My idea was that if I took any of my friends who came from any area, if they didn't like it and looked down on me, well tough luck mate. This chap opposite me... he lived in a similar sort of area, he says when he went to the Wyggeston he never took anyone home because he was always ashamed to take them home. I said, 'Hard luck mate, I'm sorry for you.' I was never ashamed of it, I was always proud of it.

City Challenge have taken steps to consult residents about what they would like to see happen and the developers are in the process of transferring some of these ideas into plans for the area, but many people have been unable to keep track of the various proposals. This has created uncertainty and has led to an exasperated, 'I'll believe it when I see it', attitude. The main concern of many residents is that while some of the ideas, such as a supermarket, will be realised, money should be spent on improving the appearance of the whole area, by improving pavements and the general infrastructure.

Except for those who still have emotional ties to the streets and houses they grew up in, the Walnut Street area is no longer seen as a desirable place to live. Better shopping facilities are vital and the International Youth House will be welcomed by many, but the major problem still to be tackled is the traffic. As one man commented, the area seems to be strangled by the road system. In effect the streets are a giant car park for the surrounding institutions.

I was moved in February 1974 and even to this day if I go in the car with my daughter and we go past where the Infirmary car park is my daughter will still... say, 'I wish we'd still got our little house down there Mum.'

The community that is described in the first half of this book can never be recreated; too much has changed locally and in society in general. Not only have streets been demolished and families moved away, there is now a huge shifting population. Students at the University and staff at the Infirmary may live in the area but they do not have a stake in the community; they are just passing through, often with a car that needs parking. Nobody is expecting City Challenge to make cars and students disappear, but with a degree of imagination it could help to make Walnut Street an area that people will want to move to rather than away from. This is the real challenge.